D1383356

DESIGN FOR DEATH

DESIGN

FOR

DEATH

BARBARA JONES

The Bobbs-Merrill Company, Inc.
A Subsidiary of Howard W. Sams & Co., Inc., Publishers
Indianapolis · Kansas City · New York

Printed in the United Kingdom
First American Edition 1967
Library of Congress catalog card number 67-24907

ACKNOWLEDGEMENT

I have had a great deal of help with this book. Many of the people who have taken trouble and spent time for me have asked to remain anonymous, but I would like to ask everyone who has been so kind to me to accept my most grateful thanks.

PHOTOGRAPHS

Frontispiece by Richard Parkinson
Page 72 by Michael Clark
Pages 102, 248, 289 by R. B. Clark-Ward
Pages 63, 112 by Gerti Deutsch
Page 285 by R. K. Freeman & Co.
Pages 222, 224, 228 by Clarence Laughlin
Pages 58, 180, 208 by Eric de Maré
Page 103 (lower) by Richard Parkinson
Pages 103 (upper) 188, 192, 195, 196, 197, 218 by the author

CONTENTS

INTRODUCTION 9

THE CORPSE 15

THE SHROUD 53

THE COFFIN 71

THE HEARSE AND THE UNDERTAKER'S SHOP 97

THE FLORAL TRIBUTES 119

PRINTING AND THE WORD 135

THE PROCESSION 159

THE CEMETERY AND THE CREMATORIUM 177

THE TOMB 203

RELICS AND MEMENTOS 235

WHERE DEATH GETS YOU 257

LOVING DEATH 277

NOTES 296

INDEX 302

BY THE SAME AUTHOR

The Isle of Wight

The Unsophisticated Arts

Follies and Grottoes

Solomon Grundy
Born on a Monday
Christened on Tuesday
Married on Wednesday
Took ill on Thursday
Worse on Friday
Died on Saturday
Buried on Sunday
This is the end
Of Solomon Grundy

TRADITIONAL

INTRODUCTION

Everyone dies. For thousands of years, uncountable millions of corpses have been given funerals, and the living have always been faced with the problems of valedictory ceremonials for the dead and what to do with the corpses. Most of them have been buried, burnt, preserved, put in the sea, or exposed to the air. Quicklime, acids, eating and shrinking are more rare, and on the whole the overtly scientific methods go with unnatural death, so that earth, air, fire, and water are the most common agents of disposal.

The choice of method and of the rituals accompanying it are governed like all human activity by unreason and reason, and by ecology, economics, religion and the differences of temperament produced by them. The main factor in any community's attitude to the dead may be *altruism,* concern for the future material or spiritual comfort of the dead by providing food or performing rituals to preserve the spirit from hostile ghosts. Or it may be *nostalgia,* concern with the lonely sorrows of the bereaved, and with recounting the virtues of the dead. Or it may be *desire to communicate* with the dead spirit, perhaps to comfort it, or to get guidance and comfort from it. Or it may be *terror,* fear of the spirit which is now inimical to the living, or dread of the tabus attached to corpses.

Or at the far end of the scale it may be *selfishness,* desire to harness the spirit for future use by the living.

Within these motives, fashions and beliefs change, become simple or complex, or run side by side; at the end of the nineteenth century twelve concurrent methods of disposal were recorded in New South Wales alone[1] – six different earth burials, exposure to the air, surface burial, tree burial, smoking, eating, and burning.

Most of the methods of disposal involve ritual, and the rituals demand artefacts. Most of the artefacts are special; there are shrouds, coffins, urns, ossuaries, food, hearses, biers, bedevilled flowers, writings, stones, monuments and graveyards, and almost everything everywhere from the funeral food to the necropolis is peculiar to death.

No one really expects to die or to have to deal with death, but suddenly it happens, and then even the most rational of the living find that it has stirred up lost scraps of ritual in them, and fired a mindless chain of trimmings and doings that are easier to accept than to refuse.

Death has been the subject of splendid words; we know that it is the great leveller, cometh soon or late, lays its icy hand on kings, supports one of the largest industries in Great Britain, and is (at least to Christians and Muslims who must regard all human activity as a way of passing the time, albeit carefully, until death) the gateway to paradise. Since death is so final, universal, and generally well-spoken of, we might expect that the things made for it would be either rich and golden or noble and stark, but no; most of the pyramids and mausoleums lie behind us, and the trappings of western death are mean and ugly. All over Europe and North America the things are much alike; and we have an odd, flat, funeral art, the thinnest possible dilution of gothic-barocco-cubist. Undoubtedly (as reason shows no advance in our affairs) it will all remain with us for many years, and is worth consideration.

The intention of this book is to look mainly at the things made today or recently in England and the United States. The other things are here for comparison, or because I like them; liking is the hard base of everything, so I have drawn what I like. The chapters follow the fairly standard pattern of what happens to the corpse; what is done to it after death, how it is wrapped up, what it is put in, its procession to the grave, its disposal and commemoration, with the various artefacts attending it; two final chapters are about things connected less with the corpse than with its effect on other people. I have left out a lot of the qualifying words – *per-*

haps, possibly, sometimes, could be, and *certain authorities consider,* because death is subject to fashion like all activities, and the hard line cannot be drawn, and we all know it.

There are two more points that crop up constantly. One is that most of the older things I have drawn were made for the funerals of rich or important people and were not used for the funerals of the poor until the undertaking trade was established in the west, when things could be hired and the lucky poor could have palls or plumes or whatever was smart at the time. The other point is that, especially in the east, many things made for death are ephemeral, and destroyed at the funeral, and so reach us only in paintings, writings, or photographs; many types of ephemera have undoubtedly been lost without trace.

Death is often symbolized, and the same symbols may be used in any one place or time on many different objects. In Europe alone it may appear as a skull or as a skull and crossbones, an hourglass (sometimes winged), a bat, a broken column, an anchor, a drooping candle, a scythe, a skeleton, an upended torch, a worm, the broken tools of a trade. Belief in resurrection can be shown as the serpent Oroburos swallowing his own tail, a phoenix, a butterfly. Mourning has symbolic plants; the evergreens, yew, cypress and bay, weeping willow, rosemary, myrtle, fir, palm, ivy, violets, lilies, wheat. Bees have an unexplained link with death; in England they were once thought to abandon the hive if no one went to tap at their door and tell them of a death in the house, and honey has been left as food for the dead wherever bees are found – similarity links funeral customs as frequently as difference separates them.

The artefacts, I have said, are now badly designed. It is easy to understand why; people are less interested in death than they used to be. In primitive societies, death is accepted and respected; it is everywhere, often violent, in the trees, in the wind, in the night. Everyone gives conscious thought to it, and the rich take great pains for rich survival after it, taking with them complete small townships for comfort. In small settled communities acceptance gets weaker, but since nothing much happens there in peacetime except farming, death has high entertainment value. Urbanization finally kills acceptance, and today death is hardly talked of, is indeed seen as top tabu subject (the elaborate rituals of America are discussed only when they must be, and then in a cloud of euphemisms). There are three main reasons for the decline of death's

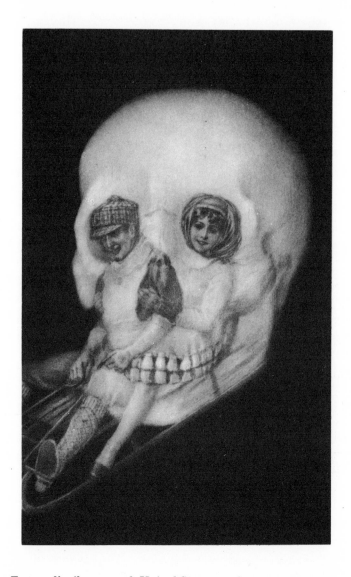

Trompe l'oeil post-card. United States, early twentieth century

prestige in the western world; first, death is further from us that it used to be – disease and starvation are beginning to be controlled, children survive, we live longer; second, everyone's life is much fuller, even if only with television; third, we now have little community life, each city family being a horrid cell on its own instead of part of a horrid whole.

– Whatever's that?
– A sheep's skull.
– Fancy having a skull about.
– You've got one in your own head.
– Morbid, I call it.

Death is a morbid subject only so far as, yes, *mori* is 'to die' in Latin and so death is rightly morbid, but for the last century morbid has meant unhealthy, and this death can hardly be said to be. Certainly, at the end of a long day in the galleries and libraries of one of the great museums, one may come to see them only as repositories of dust, but this is soon cured by leaving the museum and looking at the people outside. Look at a man and woman walking along, sidewise together. She is carrying a child, he is carrying a carrycar. His face says I have been trapped, I am a splendid male animal in a cage. I haven't a ha'porth of intelligence or virility or virtue, but I want you to know that I am a splendid male animal, caged. Her face says, I have been trapped, I am a marvellous primitive cat, or earth-mother, caged. I haven't a ha'porth of intelligence or sex or virtue, but I do want you to know that I am a leopardess, caged.

Don't undo the doors of the cages, either of them would drop down dead. They are more morbid than the corpses.

THE CORPSE

A corpse has only the rights that the living will give it, and the living have a lot of different ideas on what is to be done. In general, the corpse may be disposed of, or kept. It can be kept as itself, as like life as possible, or changed, or used as the basis for artwork, which in turn may be simple or extremely complex.

It is not an easy medium to handle. Medically, one always dies of something specific, but people do appear to die of old age, and then they begin changing long before death. The 'terminal expression', or looking like death, can be watched advancing in the geriatric wards of a hospital, where a new vocabulary goes with death, and prognosis means ETD.

The ward is full of nice clean old men; they are in pyjamas and dressing-gowns eating dinner at 11.30 in the morning round a table in the centre of the ward.

'Nurse, is there any *mince*.'

'Not today, dear.'

'Nurse, where's my *stick*?'

'It's here, dear, but you're having your nice dinner now, you won't want it yet.'

'I don't want you to fall over it, Nurse.'

Columbian mummy. Fourteenth century A.D.

'It'll be all right, I only fall over matchsticks – eat it all up, now. Don't you all look nice, all you little men?' and so they are, all little men, the dying shrink. The terminals are in bed, in comas, but reviving for a moment to be drawn, very thin, noses sharp as pins; skulls all. If the folded hands become unfolded, the old men sometimes find it difficult to get them back just right. The ears look very large and coarse.

Going

18   Gone

Laid out

The body goes on changing after death, but faster; the blood stops circulating, and gravity has therefore more effect, pulling flesh downwards into new shapes and sharpening prominent bones still further. The body gets cold quickly, and the skin colour changes from pink with green shadows to yellow with purple ones.

In some cultures these changes are accepted, and the funeral rites of ordinary people call only for an orderly arrangement of the limbs and some simple wrapping (very early burial customs often left the corpse composed in a pre-natal position. There is no evidence to show whether this was symbolic or to avoid too much digging in a hot climate). One would expect that as religions became less elaborate and demanding, so the funeral rites would become simpler, and certainly in Europe today very little is done to the body in normal circumstances; it is washed, the hair is brushed and combed, the eyes and mouth closed and the limbs straightened. The body lies on its back. A little art may be used to arrange the head 'in a natural pose' and to cross or fold the hands with the fingers lightly curled; the effect aimed at is an appearance of sleep. In some countries and classes the body is viewed by friends and relations, at home in bed or in the coffin, in church, or at the undertakers, and it may then be necessary in hot weather for the body to be lightly embalmed – or cared for, or given hygienic or sanitary or preservative treatment – endless euphemisms belittle death.

In other cultures, however, the corpse is elaborately treated and every effort is made either to give back the look of life or to give the corpse a new appearance altogether.

The new-appearance techniques are rare and usually practised in war. Some American Indian tribes went to great lengths; the Outina, for instance, scalped an enemy corpse, broke up the bones in the arms and legs to make a neat package, left it to dry in the sun and finally shot an arrow up its arse. Burial of friends and relations, however, in the earth or in a tomb on top of it, is often preceded by strenuous efforts to keep the body just like life, and the usual method is to make a mummy of it by drying or by embalming or by a mixture of the two. No satisfactory method has yet been found, and except in America most people have stopped trying.

The Ancient Egyptian mummy rightly stands in everyone's mind as the symbol of elaborate death rites and almost obsessional preservation of the corpse. During the 3,000 years of Egypt's dynastic history, beliefs changed many times. Early burial customs demanded dismemberment of the body to ensure the release of the soul; later, it was believed that the soul would live in Paradise for just so long as the mummy survived in the tomb, and perfect preservation of the corpse became an all-absorbing and expensive goal.

The hot, dry climate encouraged, or suggested, preservation; early corpses, buried curled up in the sand, remain desiccated but intact. Later, people began to bury with the dead in the sand things that would be needed in the afterlife (Paradise being a better Egypt), and gradually for the rich these grave-goods multiplied far beyond the obvious pots and weapons and clothes, to model cattle, horses, chariots, hundreds of servants, houses, and boats, filling not merely a tight grave but whole suites of tomb-chambers.[1] The preserving sand was by this time a long way from the body, and other methods had to be tried. The aim of embalming was to preserve both the body and a portrait of the dead. Early mummies had the head modelled with resinous pastes or plaster in the bandages; later, portrait masks were used instead, and portrait statues were placed in the tombs to give the dead a new lease of life through a living image.

Many methods of embalming were tried until finally a series of practices was established, with dry burial in the preserving sand still used for the poor, who could also be painted with bitumen or given the simplest form of embalming – the body was purged, and soaked in a soda solution for seventy days. By a more elaborate method, the body was chemically eviscerated with cedar oil while it soaked for seventy days in natron,[2] which dissolved the tissues so that nothing was left but skin and bone. The bodies of the rich were surgically eviscerated, and the brain and viscera separately preserved in special jars. The cavities were washed and stuffed with spices and resins before being sewn up, and then the body was soaked in soda, for seventy days. These were the mummies that were carefully wrapped in yards of cotton or linen bands, lapped during the later periods in elaborate patterns centred on gold studs. Herodotus gives an account of it all, including a description of the embalmer showing the friends of the dead a series of wooden models, exquisitely, moderately, and finally roughly made, so that the friends could choose what sort of mummy they wanted.

The Greeks washed, anointed, and clothed their corpses, and buried them with a coin in the mouth for Charon and a honeycake for Cerberus.

Sometimes there were coffins, and after about 1000 B.C. cremation came into fashion.

The Romans used both methods but on the whole cremation was used earlier and burial replaced it with the spread of Christianity. Embalming was only used when a great personage lay in state. The most interesting Roman funeral custom was that of using wax masks, careful portraits of ancestors used only for funerals and worn by actors who mimed their welcome to the new dead. He himself was represented by an actor chosen to look as like him as possible, briefed in his mannerisms and wearing a mask of him that was afterwards put away to join the ancestors at the next funeral. This use of portraits began again in the Middle Ages, as we shall see later, but wax was superseded by wood and did not become fashionable again until the seventeenth century.

During the Middle Ages important people were occasionally pickled or embalmed, following, like the Romans, the Egyptian principle of evisceration, and sometimes corpses were boiled to remove the flesh so that the bones could be safely transported. Crusaders and knights going to the wars took their own cauldrons.

Later many attempts were made to preserve corpses for dissection and medical research generally, and then, in 1618, Harvey announced his discovery of the circulation of the blood. More than a century later Dr William Hunter published the first full account of arterial embalming, which by the middle of the nineteenth century replaced all other methods. The blood is drained from the body through a vein and replaced with a formalin-based fluid through an artery. Removal of the dark blood improves the colour of the corpse and so leads on to more complicated art-work than plain washing and combing.

In modern America art-work has reached an almost Egyptian intensity, but with the difference that in Egypt everything possible was done to keep the body intact for ever without (so far as we know) any ritual of last looks, while in America the embalmed body is painted and dressed for inspection, and the embalming is unlikely to last as long as the Egyptian, though the word 'embalming', coloured by everyone's memories of the mummies in the museums, implies permanence by itself, and the size of the huge caskets and the for-ever vaults to go round them perhaps suggest enough everlastingness to justify it all, if you want to last for ever.

It took the Egyptians at least a thousand years to perfect their techniques, while American undertakers have only been embalming for just over a century. In 1886 one of them wrote[3] that the first embalming he could remember was that of a young lady who hanged herself in a wood-shed near Carlisle, Virginia, in the spring of 1853. He opened the abdomen, emptied the interior, filled the cavity of the viscera, sewed up the incision, placed the body for four weeks in a solution of water, salt, zinc chloride and alum. This turned the skin grey or red in spots, but in time most of these disappeared. The body was put on a board to dry, with several small incisions to let fluids escape, and afterwards it travelled the United States several times, ending in a vault in Peoria, Illinois, not in very good condition and never lifelike. A lot of horrors were trailed round provincial America in the nineteenth century, freaks, and corpses, and dusty little troupes of performing animals, and penny readers, and revival tents. Now the great advances in communications have killed the powerful vernacular drive to knit-up something out of nothing, like making models of Milan Cathedral with matchsticks, or decorating plates with cigar-bands, or re-inventing embalming.

The Civil War established the embalmer's art in America; draining and arterial injections were beginning to replace the long soak, and large numbers of embalmers sprang up to prepare the dead soldiers for ship-ment home when the relatives demanded it. Coffins got richer, too, and the whole curious American funeral may be said to have started with the Civil War.

By 1885, embalming was becoming a commonplace, and by the end of the century, all doubts were over, and a Lady Traveller in embalming fluids sent a carte-de-visite, 'I am coming in to see you'.

In 1900, the Massachusetts College of Embalming was set up, later advertising in England as well as America, and in 1912 Joel E. Crandall[4] of New York was offering Demisurgery to the public. His photograph shows him with hair parted down the middle, glowingly enthusiastic but calm with integrity. He tells us that he saw a man who had been killed by a train, and was so moved by the grief of the widow that he resolved to do something about it. It was difficult to find material for trial – 'so I had a sculptor make for me a rough mould of a head; then I disfigured it in many ways and tried rebuilding it to make it look natural'. He also worked on bodies in the morgue, and then the breakthrough came; a young man whose head had been smashed between the bumpers of two trains – 'I argued that I could not make it worse'.

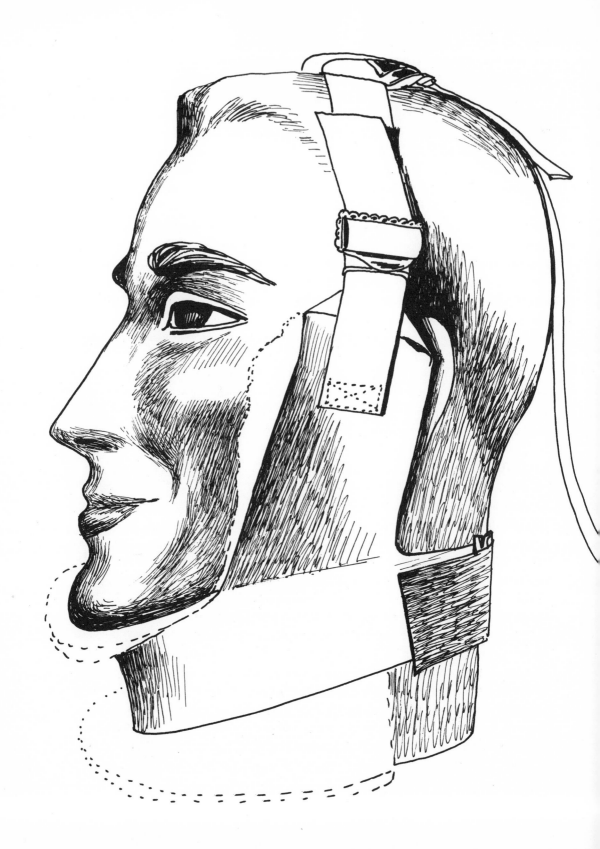

The skull was in eighty pieces, so he took it out, made a new one, and sewed the skin back again using 600 small stitches to close the cuts before the 'final moulding, filling and blending'. When the father saw the remains in the casket he said the only word that could describe the work was marvellous. Crandall was equally successful with a burned lady, three more train-crash cases, and a starved miser with cancer and maggots. Progressive photographs show a train-crash case smashed, half done, and serene in the casket. A dedicated mole, Mr Crandall.

Today, embalming is routine in America, and there are hundreds of arterial and cavity fluids, eye-caps, tissue-builders which 'will add as much as 20 lbs to the appearance of the body', sure-closes, feature-forms, electric injectors, creams, waxes, surface restorers, sealers, emollient dyes, and liquid cream cosmetics in a long range of colours from suntan through beige to moonlit blonde, so that every subject of care can look twenty years younger. The word 'mummy' is never used.

A lady, aged eighty-eight, with no relations left, has died near Chicago, and her friends have arranged care for her at a funeral home for the well-to-do. Her friends have told the undertaker that she never used much make-up and her hair just waved softly – it is newly done, pale blonde. The eyelids are held down over eye-caps (two sizes, round or oval, flesh or transparent) like Dutch-cap pessaries made of nut-meg graters. The mouth is held over padding by another fanged device, covered thickly with a heavy flush-of-youth foundation and carefully painted in with pale colours camouflaging any little awkwardnesses, rather as a Royal Academician might do it in a portrait. The prettily-tinted face looks just like plaster, as if she were a shop-dummy put in to show off the casket; the wrinkles have all been lifted, stitched away. The neck is crepey, but undoubtedly she hasn't looked so good for years. The casket is lined with ruched, bone-coloured egg-shell velvet – all the ruching was done by hand, by other old ladies. There is a ruched pillow under her head, and the right-hand half of the ruche-lined lid is down, cutting her short just below hands folded over the pubic symphysis. She is dressed in pale pink, lace over taffeta, and a little cloud of matching net hovers round her shoulders. If she had been a film star, a make-up expert and her hairdresser would have gone from the studio to help.

A gentleman, aged seventy-six, with plenty of relations left, has fallen dead in the street in Charleston, West Virginia, and his children have entrusted him to a working-class funeral home. The casket is lined with

Face-former. United States, present day

manly, maroon-coloured velvet, not ruched by the old ladies. He is in a stiff new navy-blue suit, and his shirt-collar is a little too big; the hands 'would have presented difficulties' and are not seen. He was a good-looking old man, one suspects, but is now perked quite up and heavily tanned. Undoubtedly he hasn't looked so awful for years.

These two were easy subjects, the man discoloured by his stroke, certainly, but not emaciated, swollen, or damaged. *Any* damage can be rectified, limbs restored, swollen flesh carved away – an ear lost by frostbite years ago may be replaced; it's difficult to complain of such zeal. The visible result of all the techniques is the same, a look of peaceful repose.

The skull shrines the brain, and is masked in turn by flesh; its place is vital and secret. Skulls and skeletons were honoured in the past; bones, like death generally, were well regarded, and of course their coverings of flesh dictated the plastic arts, which were representational for many centuries, pre-occupied with animal or human forms. Man loves his own image, and often makes it. Some of the images are not only realistic enough to have human hair and to appear to breathe, but are constructed like man, with an armature of wood or metal instead of bones, and a covering of wax or clay instead of flesh – one wonders if a skeleton has ever been used as armature, and if realism would be easier or more difficult. Probably from anthropomorphism, the arts in advanced societies have tended to cover up their structures; architecture was covered with carving and cladding, music became padded as soon as the right instruments were invented to do it, poetry and prose are easily embedded in qualifying clauses, and paint is a cover-up by its nature. Today, though, western sculpture and architecture show their bones.

The skull has always been top bone; it holds the brain, important in most cultures, it has a neat shape, and it looks human, except that its eyes are bigger and it laughs all the time, very sexy. Some fine things have been done with skulls, but the skull loses prestige as an image when death loses its importance – it is hardly with us now; only in Mexico does death still have a Day. Also, all symbols lose impact by repetition, like the eye, the globe, and the cross, but it is easy to see how brilliant and terrifying a symbol of death the skull once was, the intimate warm casket of ourselves exposed at last with holes for eyes and a long laugh with the lips gone. Over the years, it has lost its lower jaw and acquired two crossed thighbones, and it remains with us as the symbol for piracy rather than

Embalmed. United States, present day

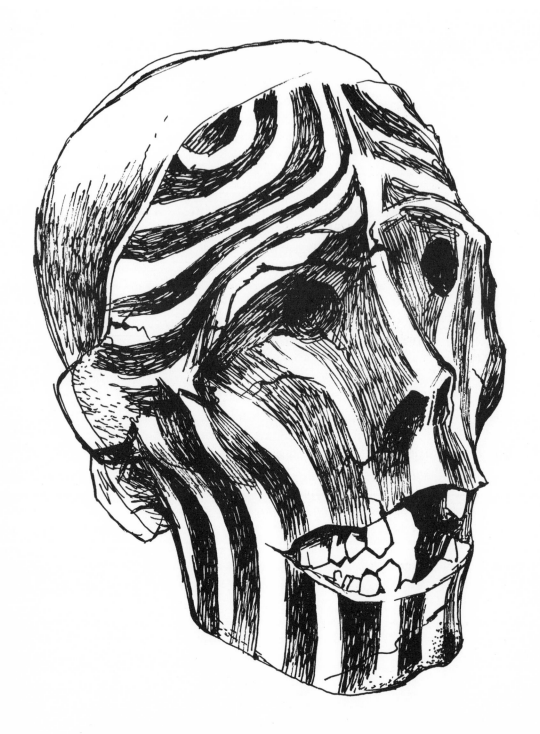

Above. Skull, artificially deformed in childhood, modelled in clay and painted. South Malekula, New Hebrides

Right. Skull kept in memory of the dead; restored and decorated with red and black clay, beads and rags. Torres Straits

Above. Skull decorated with clay and painted. String hair, cowrie eyes. Lower Sepik River, New Guinea

Right. Skull decorated with shells, incised lines, and nose ornament. Western Papua

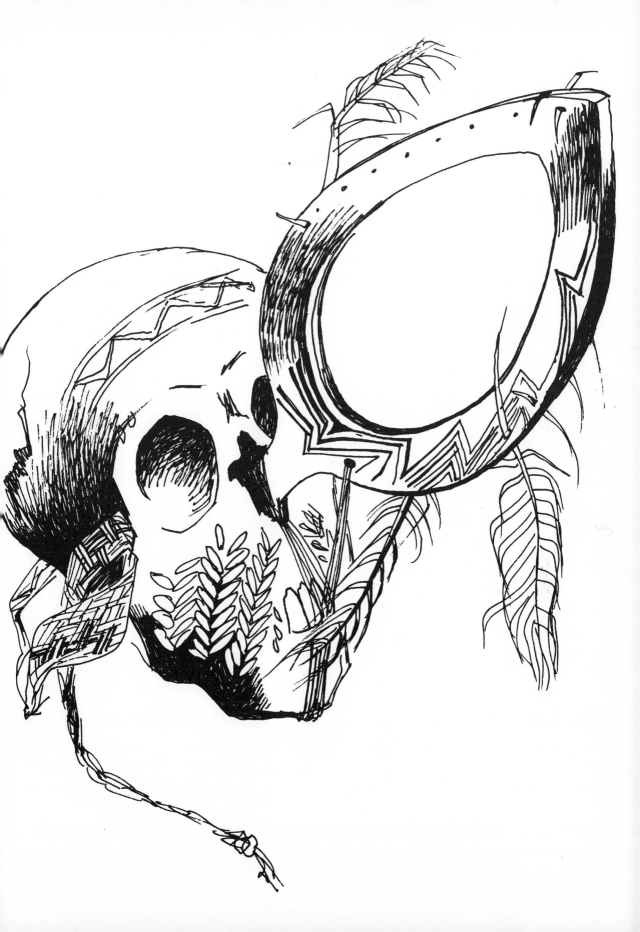

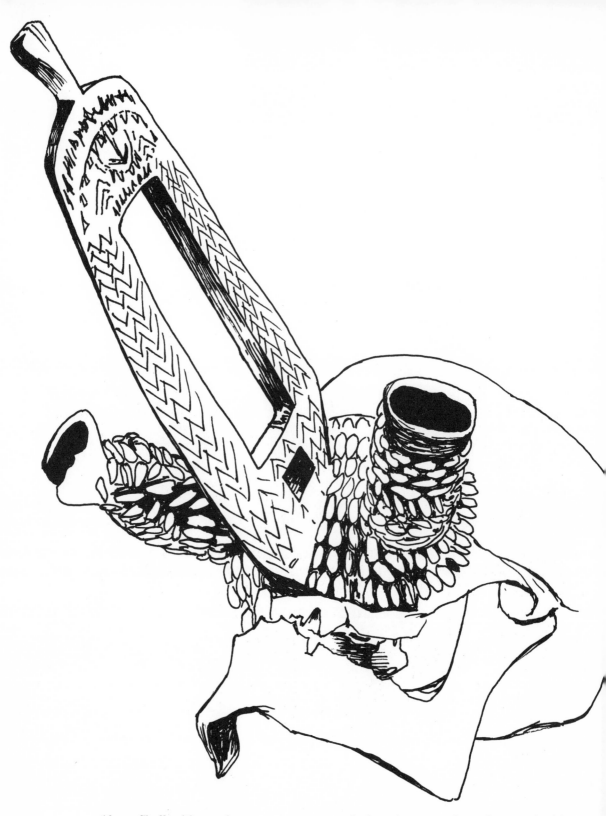

Above. ·Skull with wooden nose ornament and plugs in eye sockets, decorated with cowries. Papua

Right. The skull of a rain-maker, decorated with clay, paint, and small shells, kept by a living rain-maker to help with his work. New Ireland

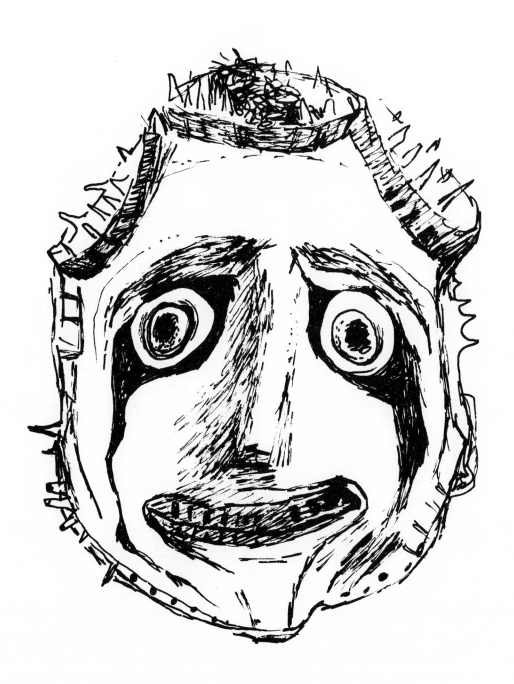

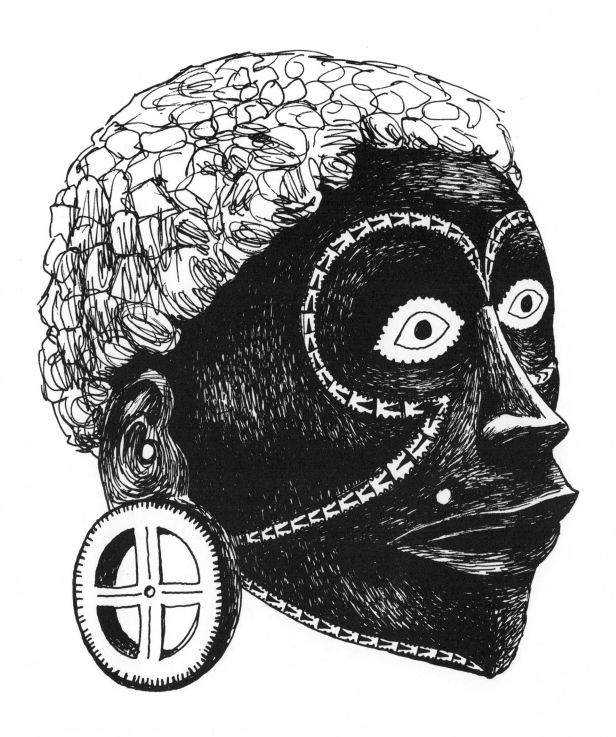

Above. Skull decorated with clay, fibre, and shell. Solomon Islands

34   *Right.* Preserved head, tattooed during life. New Zealand

death and as a warning on high-tension cables and poison bottles. But before this now universal devaluation, skulls and heads were often given great importance and treated apart from the body. The oldest we have are the beautiful neolithic skulls from Jericho, made about 7,000 years ago. Pottery had not been invented there when these were made, but clay was used to model the features of the dead on the skull itself, which was then buried under the floor of the house. In Europe skulls were occasionally cleaned and painted, but in South America and the Pacific they were used as the basis for some superb decorative work.

The shrunken heads made by the Jivaro Indians are probably the most famous death's heads, sufficiently beloved to be reproduced in plastic and nylon to hang in the back window of the car, but the original *tsantsas* are as beautiful as they are strange. The custom of shrinking was once wide-spread in South America, and the heads were described by one of Pizarro's men in 1527; the Jivaros kept the custom up longer than the other tribes, and there are many eye-witness accounts of the way they worked.

The heads were taken from enemies killed in formal forays between neighbouring villages. Endless blood-feuds were kept up until both sides got tired, when a lance would be buried for a truce, but whoever felt like feuding again could dig up the lance after twenty-four hours' notice. Before an attack, friends were rounded up for drinks and a feast, all the men painted themselves black and put on their richest ornaments, and the shaman got everyone worked up till dawn when they tried to launch a surprise attack on the rival stockade, which was fortified with traps, barricades and trenches. If the attackers broke in, they killed all small children, all the old, all the adult men, and some of the women. The heads were taken very carefully, with lance blades. The first cuts were made in a deep 'V' on the chest and the skin was peeled back till the bottom of the neck could be severed; then the heads were wrapped in leaves and put safely in baskets. The house was utterly looted and destroyed, the garden ruined and the remaining women taken to join the march home. At a safe distance, the party stopped at a suitable place offering sand, rocks and shelter, and everyone lit a fire and unpacked his head. First, the hair was parted and a cut made up the back of the neck to the widest part of the skull. More cuts were made at eyes, nose, and ears and then the skin could be peeled off and scraped. The eye slits were sewn up, the skin turned right-side-out again and three wooden pins put through the

Stuffed head, with jawbone used as necklace. Western Papua

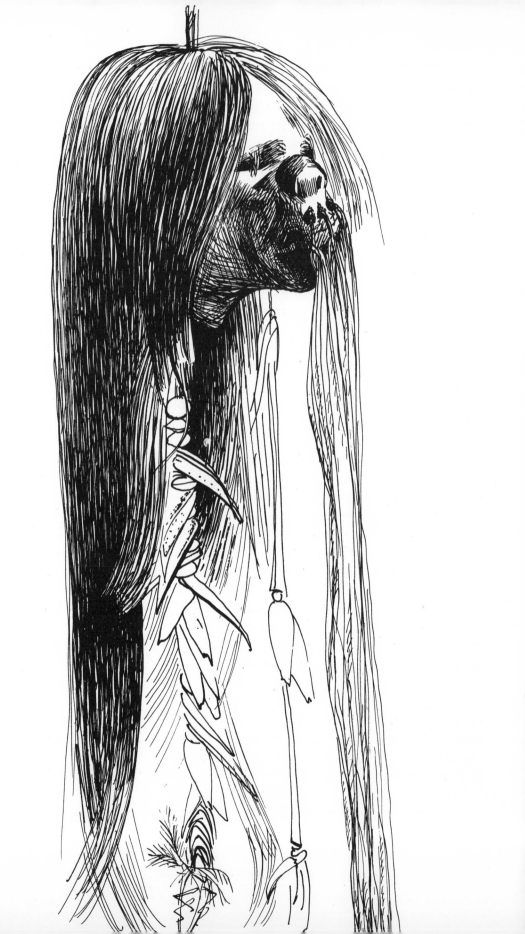

lips with strings wound round to keep the lips closed. The skin was then boiled for two hours in a large pot of water while the shrinker collected stones and heated them. During the boiling, the skin shrank to one third of its original size and became pale and rubbery. The back slit was sewn up, the head held upside down, and the largest hot stone was dropped in down the neck. The head was spun quickly to keep the stone moving and it sizzled away curing the skin, while the shrinker polished and moulded the outside with another, smaller, stone. The skin went on shrinking, and progressively smaller stones were used, always outside as well as in, and the brows and lashes were plucked out to keep scale. At the end of several hours, hot sand was used instead of stones to ease out the creases, the facial hair was singed off, the crown pierced to take a loop of fibre and the neck sewn round. Now it was evening, and bigger fires were lit with the heads strung above them to smoke. They got very black and hard and the unsleeping men polished them up with cloths. At dawn, a man ran ahead to alert the village, and the women killed a chicken for each *tsantsa,* catching the blood in a bowl. The men stuck their *tsantsas* on lances in the ground, and stood beside them while the women painted spots of blood on their right legs and the juice of *Genipa americana,* their black warpaint, on the left. The exhausted men sank down on their beds and smeared their chests with blood, and everyone had a great feast, with a dance to mime the killings. The captured women wept, or got proxies to weep for them, and everyone had a thoroughly emotional time. Then the *tsantsas* were wrapped up and either buried or hung over the bed, and each man who had collected a head began a life of rigid discipline for six months, with no sex and a diet that excluded the flesh of all fierce birds, animals and fish; a bland time.

Fakes. The Jivaro sometimes shrank the heads of sloths if a real head was not available for any reason, and sloths, or monkeys, are still done for the tourist trade, which also absorbed for many years the heads of the unclaimed dead in hospitals. Today's fakes are made of monkey or dog-skin soaked and stretched over moulds, and it is said that they can be detected because they mistakenly have eyebrows, and both the eyebrows grow the same way.

Sometimes the corpse is carried on the coffin in effigy in the form of a skeleton to emphasize death, or a living image to minimize it. The image may be dressed in velvet and jewels, like the effigies made for the English royal funerals between 1272 and 1625. When a king's power is absolute, his birth and death must be absolute too, and most societies under hereditary rule make sure that the corpse is seen by a lot of people to prevent imposture later. Violence attends power, too; the deaths and funerals of the Norman and early Plantagenet kings were rough. William II: *pauci rusticanorum cadaver, in rheda caballaria compositum, Wintoniam in episcatum devexere, cruore undatim per totam viam stillante* – carried to Winchester in a wagon with the blood dripping in a wavy line all the way. Henry I was disembowelled and roughly embalmed by a skilful butcher before the body was taken to Caen. Henry II was richly dressed and carried in procession with his face uncovered for the people to see, and blood ran from his nose. Henry III, though, had it peaceful; he was dressed in crown and robes and put in a coffin, covered. The bills refer to 300 lbs of wax used for the funeral, and accounts say how splendid the king looked, so possibly some of the wax was used for an effigy, though the two whole figures, two busts, and three heads left in the Abbey are all of wood, and other bodies that survived till World War II were leather. The earliest ones, Edward III and Katherine de Valois, consort of Henry V, are whole figures made of wood, hollowed at the back for lightness. Edward is a rough figure without hands or feet to which his death mask of linen and plaster was fastened, with hair and a beard now gone; his face shows the distortion of the stroke from which he died. Katherine, who died in childbirth in Bermondsey, has carved, red-painted robes and a head carved from a death-mask with a groove for the crown, and the artist could not or would not restore the semblance of life; her expression is very terminal indeed. Henry died in France and had a '*representation de cuyr bouilly painct moult gentillement*'. Edward IV: 'in y^t herce above ye corps was upon the cloth of golde abovesaid a personage lyke to the symilitude of ye Kinge in habit Royall crowned w^t a crown of his head, holding in one hand a scepter and in the other hand a ball of sylver & gylt w^t a cross paty'.

Anne of Bohemia's fine head, carved from a death-mask, has lost what was probably a wooden body, but the later effigies were differently made with wooden or plaster heads and hands, and bodies made of stuffed leather, plaster, or cloth on rigid frames. There is a bust of Anne of Denmark, exquisitely carved and painted, a dull plaster head of Mary Tudor and a good pair for Henry VII and his wife Elizabeth of York. Henry's head is a death-mask, most brilliantly executed. His plaster body

Effigy of Katherine de Valois, d. 1437. Westminster Abbey, London

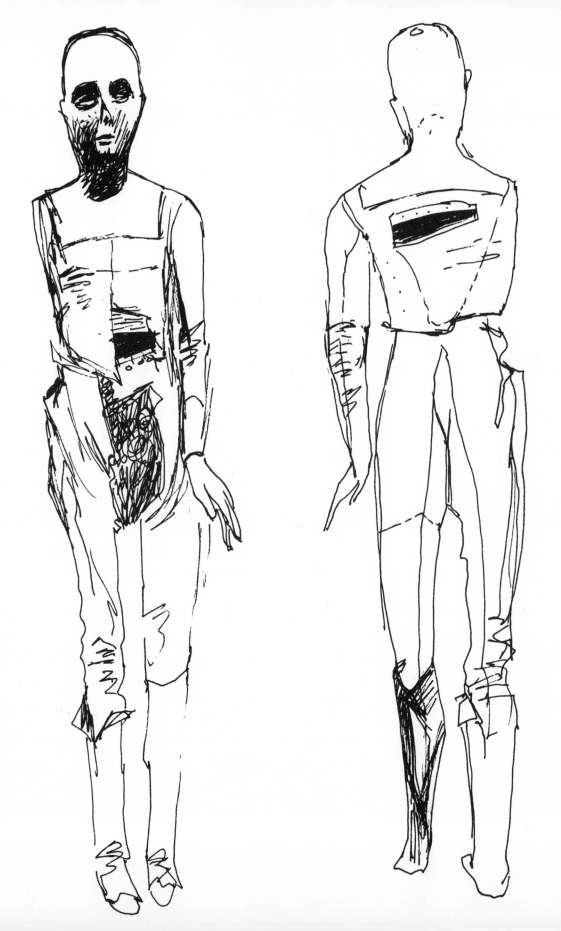

Effigies of Elizabeth of York (*left*) d. 1503, and (*above*) Henry Prince of Wales, son of James II. From photographs; effigies destroyed except for head and hand

43

was stuffed with hay which has now been identified as twelve plants from the fields outside London; the Kinge Pyctour cost £6 12*s* 8*d*. Elizabeth's effigy is the most completely documented of them all. She died in the Tower in 1503 and ten days later the corpse was taken to the Abbey on a 'chayre which was new pareled as foloeth. Furst all the baylles, sydes and coffres covered with black velvet & over all along of a pretty depnes a cloth of black velvet with a crosse of cloth of sylver.' The horses were caparisoned in black velvet, and the coffin was made of holly-wood 'whereon was an ymage or personage lyke a quene, clothed in ye very robes of estate of ye quene having her very ryche crowne on her hed her here about her shoulder, hir scepter in her right hand & her fyngers well garneshed w^t ryngs of golde and p^{r}syous stones and on every end of ye chayre on ye cofres kneled a gentleman hussher by all the way to West-minster'.

The bills are very detailed, starting with the 'pikture', which needed two waynscotts called Regall 2*s* 4*d*, one waynscot borde, ii pece of peretre tymber price 8*d*, two joyners for half a day and the hole night, nails, glue, and seven small shepeskynnes for the body 2*s* 4*d*. The hair was hired for 5*s*, nine yards of crimson satin were used for the robe which was bordered with black velvet, and an undergarment was made of yellow satin. Item to Mr Lawrence for kerving of the hedde with Fredrik his mate 13*s* 4*d*, item to Wechon Kerver and hans van hoof for kerving of the twoo hand 4*s*. For the priming coat 4*d*, and to master Henry for painting of the image 4*s*. The hearses were huge and elaborate, one at the Tower and another at the Abbey, with thousands of candles. The paints are listed, gold, silver, bisse, russet, vermylon, verdigris, gold and silver foil, it is all listed down to the packthread.

The last effigies made were of James I, his son Henry, Henrietta Maria for burial at St Denis, and, oddly, of General Monck, in armour. More oddly still James I, carved by Maximilian Colt, was also in armour, with a crown which broke and was replaced by a better crown. The vogue for the Middle Ages had hardly started when James died in 1625 – was his taste more sophisticated than one had thought or was it someone else's idea? In any case, it set no precedent; his was the last effigy of this sort.

Meanwhile the earlier, outmoded, effigies were neglected. Seven of them were refurbished for a visit from King Christian of Denmark, but by 1682 they were in the upper part of Bishop Islip's chapel in the Abbey (shoved up there, one supposes, at the time of the Protectorate) – a drawing of 1786 shows eight of them in the Henry V chantry, derelict and mostly naked. By 1872, another drawing has them back in the chapel, crowned, haphazard bundles crammed into a cupboard and named the Ragged Regiment. During World War II they were stored for safety in the undercroft but this was flooded after bombing and by the time restoration started in 1949 the leather, plaster, and hay were rotted beyond hope. Today we have seven remarkable portraits, but the fascination of the disintegrating images can only be seen in old photographs.[5]

Charles I and Cromwell did not have state funerals, and when Charles II died, sixty years after James I, taste had changed, and a very fine waxwork of Charles was made and dressed in Garter robes. It had some connection with the funeral but was not carried on the coffin. Wax effigies were fashionable for about a hundred years, and the Abbey has eleven of them. Charles II, the Duchess of Richmond, and the Duchess of Buckingham and her sons were all made for funerals and were stood beside the tombs. La Belle Stuart had her favourite parrot stuffed and he is still there on a perch. Queen Elizabeth is an eighteenth-century pop re-hash of the effigy shown in the obit rolls (see page 159), and was made when the original robes were reduced to a ruff. William and Mary and Anne, William Pitt and Nelson were simply added to the collection to keep up public interest in the waxworks. Pitt's head in a box is good, and cleaning has revealed nice details – the black velvet backing to the Duchess of Buckingham's jewels was stiffened with cut playing cards – but the best of them are Charles II, and the Nelson commissioned from Catherine Andras as a counter-attraction to the tomb and funeral-car in Saint Paul's.

In France, the royal effigies became more important than the kings. The effigy for the funeral of Henry Vth of England in 1422 was made in France, and when Charles VI died two months later, the French copied the idea, making *le mole du corps, des jambes et des bras faict de fustaines et toiles pour estre plus fermes*. The head and hands were ambiguously *apres le vif . . . le plus proprement que on a peu*. Two death masks were made for the effigy of Charles VII, which was dressed exactly like the corpse inside the coffin, in a blue robe covered by a blue velvet mantle with a deep ermine collar, a silver crown on the head, the hands holding the sceptre and the hand of justice. But when Charles VIII and the rest of the kings were later exhumed, they were found naked in the coffins, and until 1610 when the custom ended with the funeral of Henri IV, the effigies were the continuing monarchy of France.

For the funeral of François I, Clouet himself made the death mask and two pairs of hands, one pair praying for the lying-in-state (where also the effigy had supplanted the corpse), and one pair to hold the sceptre and hand of justice for the procession. The effigy lay in state crowned in royal robes, and for eleven days wine and food were served to its place at a table by the bed with a cardinal to bless the meal. The hangings of the room were blue and gold for a month, and were then changed overnight to black; the coffined corpse under a splendid pall replaced the effigy so that the new king could visit the corpse instead of the doll – two kings of France together would not do.

For the procession, the coffin lay under its pall on a wagon drawn by six horses in black caparisons. Behind came the insignia and thirty-three bishops. The effigies of two of François' sons who had died before him were carried by their gentlemen, and then, behind more dignitaries, the spurs, the palfrey of estate, and the Master of the Horse with the sword of France. The salt-carriers of Paris, whose ancient privilege it was to bear the body of the king, carried the effigy on a litter hung with cloth-of-gold. The canopy went behind so that the effigy could be clearly seen – all the attention of the crowd and the squabbles of officials to be in places of honour were directed to it. Few of the people could have ever seen the living king in robes and crown, and the waxwork in state held the day.

Wax is a better medium for mimicking death than life – it looks like dead flesh with little further effort – and some good figures survive in Europe; there is a fine one in S. Maria della Vittoria in Rome, under the altar opposite Bernini's Teresa, livid wax in blue and white satin, a saint or martyr stabbed in the throat. The Hermitage in Leningrad has a Peter the Great case, with his death-mask and a wax bust flanking a figure of the Czar by the elder Rastrelli, wax on wood, sitting large as life in his own hair and his own clothes, much like Jeremy Bentham in London.

An effigy may still preside at a funeral; in 1965 Professor Griaule, a French ethnologist, died in Paris and was buried there. For twenty-five years he had worked with the Dogon in the Sudan, and when the body was not brought back for a chieftain's funeral, the Dogon made two effigies of Griaule; one, dressed in his own clothes, was set up on a chair by a table to watch the other, warmed by the skin of a sacrificed ram, being carried to burial.[6]

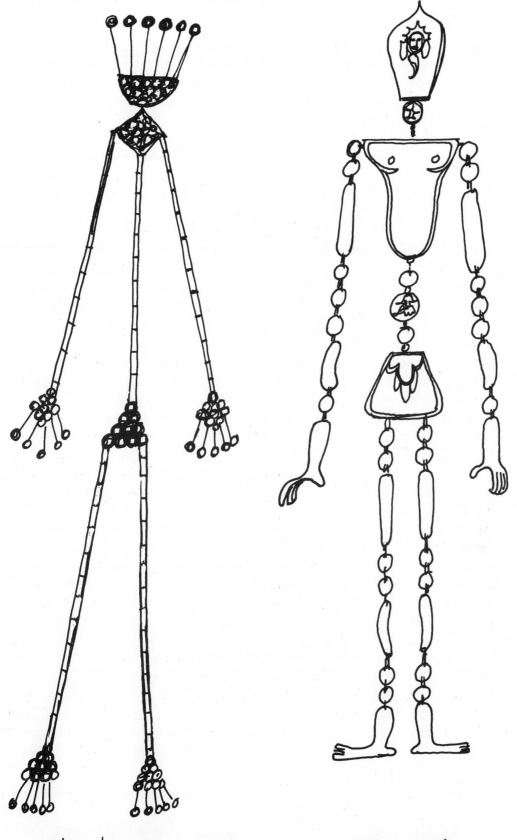

uku kepeng   BALI   uku selaka

All over the world, images are company for the dead. In Bali, the *uku kepeng* is a death-size doll, a stylized skeleton made of yarn with old Chinese coins representing the bones. *Uku selaka* is a richer version, kept as an heirloom and not interred, made of silver plaques on silver wire, or gold on gold.

In Kafiristan, an eastern district of Afghanistan, magnificent wooden effigies are still occasionally set up in the graveyards, larger than life, women in horned head-dresses, men in turbans, on horses, two horses, or thrones. Effigies are used twice in Kafiristan funerals. The first one is made of straw at the time of the death. The corpse and the effigy are both dressed in bright silks, with jewellery for women and cross-belts and daggers for men. Feathered sticks are stuck in the turban and boot-tops. After a day of ritual dancing, the corpse is carried in a rectangular wooden coffin to the graveyard on a hillside above the village, where it is propped among the rocks. The effigy is kept in the village to be kissed by the mourners with more dancing and feasting, as money allows. Afterwards the doll is stripped of its silks and burnt in the cemetery.

One year after the funeral the wooden effigy goes up. Effigies are cut with axe and knife and have fierce faces with white stones for eyes and slit mouths. Real turbans are sometimes bound over the carved onion-dome ones, with sprigs of evergreen tucked under them. The horses are thin and worried, and the effigies sit astride with their hands stiffly up beside the horses' ears, staring straight ahead.

Smaller effigies which are said to be those of notable fighters are sometimes set up in the forests on square poles which are notched across the front to tally the killings.[7]

The preservation of the bodies of animals for burial was common in Ancient Egypt, where the sacred animals such as cats, hawks and crocodiles were sometimes embalmed as carefully as humans and similarly wrapped in linen cloths and bands. Pets are sometimes embalmed before burial in America today, and animals are often preserved for the home, either complete or as skins. The thin skins of humans defy, so far as I know, preservation in any way that would allow them to be kept sitting about in a favourite armchair in a characteristic pose, and they seem to be confined to bookbindings and lampshades, with tattooed specimens rating high. The skins of animals, though, are mostly thick, scaly, or covered with hair or fur, and can be taken off the corpses, cured, and

Carved wooden effigies. Kafiristan

stretched over plaster models (the newest technique), or over wood-and-wire armatures in poses of defiance, alertness or submission, for big game, small game, or pets to sit by the fire.[8] Taxidermy became increasingly fashionable from about the end of the sixteenth century, until by the second half of the nineteenth century every small town had its taxidermist's shop and most good homes their specimens, either as simple works of art or as memorials or as records of a notable bag or catch.

Freak animals were stuffed too, in the cause of science,[9] and any large animal with a hard-wearing coat could be made into a rug. The body was slit up the stomach and down the insides of the legs, then cured and spread out flat, on a piece of scarlet or green felt pinked round the edges. The skin of the head could be flattened out as part of the rug or given glass eyes and put back on to the skull; some rugs had the jaws snarled open with a plaster mouth and tongue. Bears, lions and tigers made the best rugs and sometimes got their own back when a careless visitor tripped over the head.

Many stuffed animals went into natural history museums, great treasure-houses of death, where all the animals except man, who usually appears only as a skeleton, are lovingly preserved in their skins as they never lived. No two nations prepare or mount animals in quite the same way. Two extremes are shown by museums in Stockholm and Venice. Stockholm has a lovely little Biological Museum built into a black and white timber building. At the end of a simple hall is a tender anthropomorphic group, a huge brown bear on her hind legs with one cub held up and the other held by a paw. Directly behind her rises a superb double-circle wooden staircase which gives at two levels on to stages from which to view an all-the-way-round panorama of Sweden's animals, birds, trees, mosses, ferns and flowers. Rocks are lined with auks and guillemots whose real stuffed ranks fade into painted ranks; every skill has been used to re-create the natural scene.

In Venice, there is the Museo da Storia Naturale in the Fondaco de'Turchi which I visited on an idle Sunday morning simply to see how Italians stuff badgers. The entrance is daunting, utterly bare with a couple of boring tree-sections. Up a floor, and there indeed is badger, first exhibit, rocking on upcurved Turkish toes. Beside him, an Arctic bear is in a state of thorough collapse.

Then a splendid room, one hunter's trophies, one of each. A rhino with his horns standing on his skull like dunce's caps, a legless ostrich looms from the wall with wings displayed, large elephant's ears are mounted on small elephant's feet.

In another room is a pancaked gorilla, prepared in reverse, slit up the spine instead of the belly and nailed out flat on the wall. The head is in heavily varnished 3 D, black face and eyes, burnt-sienna teeth, dried-blood lips. Across the bald chest is a curved brass plate – 'Gorilla'. He is special, and so is the Raccolta Miani, the dark fruits of an expedition to the source of the Nile in 1859: a tortoise skin, the dried head of a camel, tongue out, scars sewn up all over the skin, a desiccated crocodile in a low flat case, and, in a flatter case, a varnished black desiccated man in a stained shroud. The toes are tied together, and parts of the face have escaped the varnish. A bad room.

Then, lovely rooms of beautiful dissections, throat of ostrich, heart of hawk, marine specimens white on blue glass, the skeletons of fishes, and a whole wall lined with bottles, thin, fat, tall, short, white on blue, gold, pink, rose and azure – fish tails, whole fish, fish intestines, and an incredible white case full of sting rays, shiny siennas and golds, dissected on black boards. The white respiratory systems of snails are mounted on blood-red glass; some of the most beautiful things in Italy are in this museum.

overstuffed pin in Industrial Museum
St. Etienne

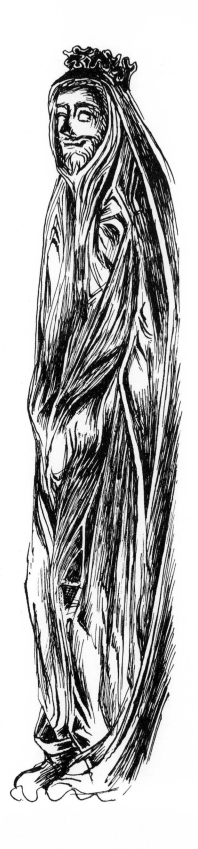

THE SHROUD

The corpse, plain, distorted or preserved, is usually covered up. It may be dressed in the clothes worn during life, or in special clothes, or wound in a sheet or a shroud or in elaborate bandages, and it may wear a portrait mask and jewels.

The treatment of the corpse itself is no guide to its wrappings, and in this the two great embalming cultures stand poles apart; Ancient Egyptian corpses, embalmed for eternal preservation, were wrapped in hundreds of yards of fine linen bands, while American corpses, embalmed for display, wear contemporary dress.

Even simple wrappings may carry special funerary patterns or be made in special colours. The colours for death include black and purple in Christian countries, white in China and Japan, blue or violet in Turkey, and some sorrowful greys and browns. When we are well we can enjoy *comédie noire,* and eat black foods, steak charred outside, mushrooms, black puddings, pickled walnuts, strong dark chocolate, all washed down with nourishing stout. Ill, we turn to milk and milk puddings, arrowroot, rice, yoghourt, bread-and-butter, pale toast, and water. At a funeral, the quick are in black, carried in black cars, the dead are in white shrouds and will lie under white marble slabs. Black is for the strong.

Left. English shrouds: Woman's shroud, 1910, and John Donne's tomb in St Paul's, London, d. 1631.
Above. Woven mask for a false head: from a Peruvian mummy-bundle

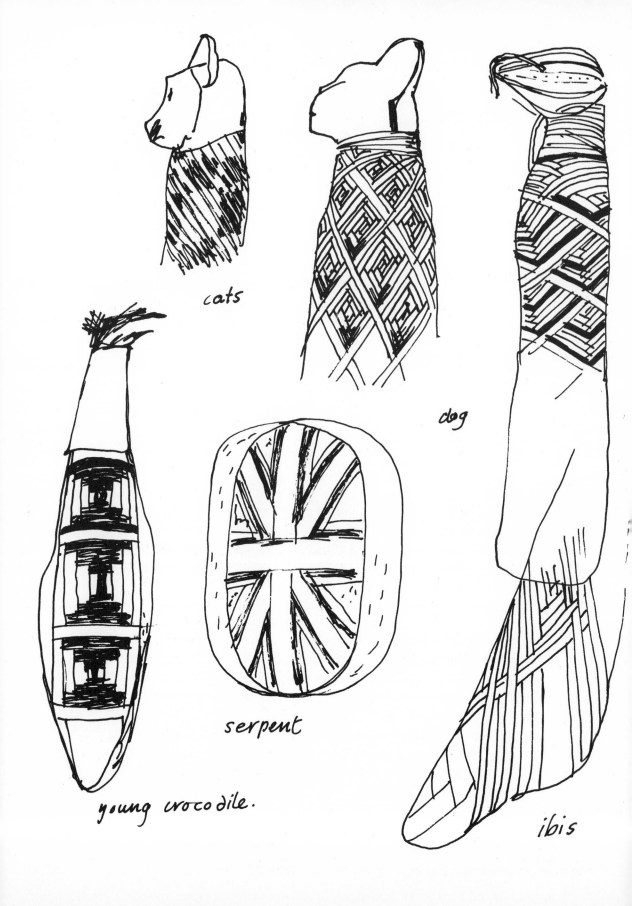

cats

dog

young crocodile.

serpent

ibis

Left. Different ways of wrapping mummified animals. Ancient Egypt. *Above.* The body of a chief of the Fali tribe, Nigeria, wrapped for burial, first in strips of rawhide, then of cotton

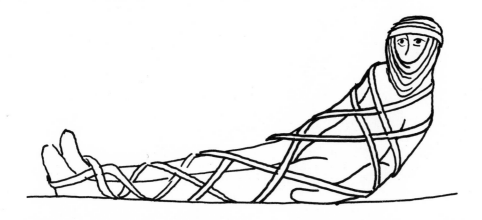

In Europe during the Middle Ages, coarse linen shrouds, or winding sheets, were in general use, and most of the poor were buried in them without a coffin. Shrouds are poetically sable, but I have not been able to find reference to them actually being black, though they were later embroidered in black, and gradually became more elaborate, first frilled, and then cut like shirts or shifts. The rich were wrapped in cerecloths, fine fabrics which had been soaked or painted with an adhesive substance such as wax – used here not to imitate flesh but to hold the cloth closely to it. An account of the opening of the coffin of Edward I, who died in 1307, says that the 'inmost covering seems to have been a very fine linen cerecloth, dressed close to every part of the body, and superinduced with such accuracy and exactness, that the fingers and thumbs of both the hands had each of them a separate and distinct envelope of that material. The face, which has a similar covering fitted thereto, retained its exact form, although part of the flesh appeared somewhat wasted.'[1] It is probably a cerecloth carved round John Donne, shivering on his urn in St Paul's, his body sagging at the pelvis as a new corpse curiously does. Outside the fine clinging folds is another wrapping like a hooded cloak, stiffened over the head, very like the contemporary mourning head-dresses of great ladies. The monument reflects the pleasure taken in gloom during the sixteenth and seventeenth centuries by educated Europeans. The long wars of the Middle Ages were over and the simpler pleasures of peace were soon exhausted. Men turned to metaphysics and melancholy. Dark images coloured poetry, Sir Thomas Browne wrote *Urne Buriall,* and mourning was fashionable. Fashions changed, too, and the winding sheets and cerecloths followed ordinary dress more closely. An Act of 1666 laid down that the dead must be buried in English wool and never in

Left. Mummy bundle with mask and head-dress of featherwork (the upper jaw can be seen under the mask). Wrappings of wool, resist-printed in blue, yellow and red. Peru, *c.* A.D. 1300. *Above.* Corpse wrappings, probably France, eleventh century A.D.

57

imported linen. A thin bays called flannel was used, and the shirt was modish, 'purfled about the Wrists, and the slit of the shroud down the breast done in the same manner. When these Ornaments were not of Woollen Lace, they are at least edg'd, and sometimes embroider'd with black Thread.'[2] The shirt was long, and tied in a tuft below the feet with wool thread. There was a cap on the head, a broad chin cloth, gloves, and a cravat; wool was not to be so all-embracing again until Dr Jaeger's day. The Act was repealed in 1815, and linen came back into favour; for one thing, it was not attacked by moths, and so some households, especially in the country, had a nicely embroidered shroud or two always in reserve. Or a linen sheet would be used, wrapped closely round the body, turned under the feet and arranged in a simple ruff round the face.

Corpses are still sometimes laid out like this in England today, but the fashion is for ordinary night clothes, or a shroud. There are of course minority customs such as those of the Cypriot communities, where the dead are buried in full outdoor clothes, hat, shoes and gloves, covered by a sheet in the centre of which a hole has been burned, never cut, for the head. For most people, though, either best nightdresses or pyjamas are laid out by the survivors, or the undertaker will provide a shroud, which he will call robe or gown.

The shrouds of the nineteen-sixties are in fact so changed from the elegant ruffles of John Donne as to *need* another name. Clothes for the living mostly do up at the front; these all tape up at the back, and the front simulates night-clothes to assist the illusion of sleep. For women, there are long-sleeved nightdresses, decorated with the mean deflated frills of the underclothing made in the nineteen-thirties for small family drapers to sell to old ladies, though there is no evidence that old ladies ever liked them. The colours are mostly pastel; ivory, cream, white, palest blue, pink or green, plain or sprigged with pale little flowers or trimmed with narrow lace. Roman Catholics favour brown.

There are also dressing-gowns. These are often white with pastel-coloured revers which do not cross over but meet at the waist just above a tasselled rayon-cord bow. They are thus sexless, but differenced at the neck by a buttonless sham pyjama front for men and a Peter-Pan collar for women. There are, of course, innovations; the newest dressing-gowns for men are made of gay paisley, properly crossed in front, with cravats of pale yellow rayon, for Sunday-morning drinkies in the tomb.

In America, the fashionable thing is afternoon dress for women and

Lady Hoby in mourning clothes on her tomb at Bisham on the Thames. Her ghost, in negative tones, is said to haunt Bisham Abbey for grief that she beat one of her sons to death

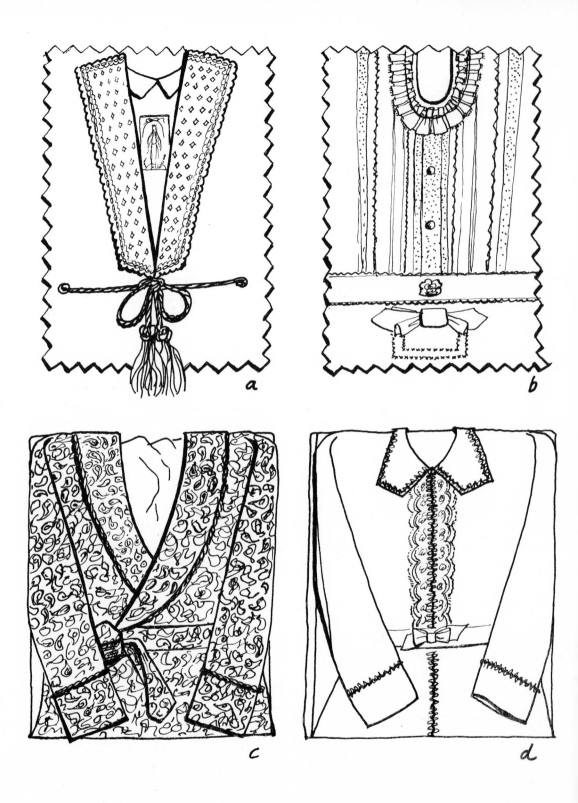

Above. Shroud samples. (*a*) Man's, Roman Catholic, brushed cotton faced with rayon. With a round inner collar, can be used for a woman. (*b and d*) Woman's, rayon with braid and ribbon. (*c*) Man's. Bright paisley-patterned rayon, pale yellow stock. All sold in England, present day. *Right.* Women's shrouds. United States, present day and late nineteenth century.

a dark suit for men. The dresses all fasten up the back but are otherwise ordinary, though to be ordinary to all women, fat, thin, fair, dark, old, young, rich, poor, WASP or Black Muslim, they are made in styles rarely seen on the living – in chiffon, crepe or lace-over-taffeta, and in pastel shades (perhaps with a matching, softening stole or net for the shoulders), the skirts and sleeves long and limp. They are like the unobtrusive evening dresses of ladies-in-waiting. Underneath are stockings, bra, falsies if needed, slip, and panties. For true care there must be shoes, pastel again, in broad and universal fittings, with gussets at the back.

It is also possible to buy animal shrouds at the pet cemeteries in America; this has not become a European fashion though undoubtedly many dogs and cats everywhere are lovingly wrapped in a piece of silk or cloth before burial in the garden – the instinct to keep the earth away is very strong.

The bereaved as well as the corpses have often worn special clothes, though this custom is dying out all over the world. The clothes were often different from ordinary ones in design, cloth, or colour, and rigid conventions governed them and the length of time for which they were worn and for whom.

Clearly such clothes, like all the other rituals of death, were something for the rich. The poor – most people – used flowers or small favours or dye. Some tribes of South American Indians infused berries to make a strong black dye that lasted through many washings, and stained their skins with it. Wives, husbands, children, sisters and brothers were painted from head to foot, second-degree relatives on legs, feet, arms, hands, and parts of the face; third-degree relatives only had black hands and feet and spots on the face.[3]

In Europe, the mourner's clothes became elaborate like the shrouds. By 1532 'mourning' meant the 'wearing of black clothes, etc, as a manifestation of sorrow for the death of a friend' (SOED), and by 1654 it meant also the clothes themselves. Black clothes. Some of them were very splendid, black velvet and sables, and were not only kept from one death to another but also handed down in the family. Later, fashion changed faster and the clothes were less rich; by the beginning of the nineteenth century there are fashion plates for mourning clothes, and black crape (a fabric that became peculiar to death) spread through all the ramifications of mourning, deep mourning, half mourning, two years, one year,

Mourning in Austria, present day

six months, one month. Larousse in 1870 printed (for the benefit of future archaeologists) correct mourning for a widow in France, one and a half years. '*Les quartre premiers mois et demi, grand deuil; robe de laine en cachemire, mérinos, cachemire d'Ecosse, pluie de laine, baarpoor, drap Zéphir, drap Chambord, drap impérial, drap d'Orléans, drap d'Alep, drap Montpensier, drap amazone, Valencia croisé, stoff, orléans, batiste de laine, tamise, escot, anacoste, voile: mousseline laine, barège uni, Zalamine, satin de Chine, croisé coton, bijoux de jais.*'[4]

In England, mourning increasingly muffled the increasing middle classes and spread on downwards until by the end of the nineteenth century all but the very poorest had a bit of black to hand. Black borders ran round handkerchiefs and writing-paper, wider and wider. There were black cockades for coachmen's hats, and black draperies for drums at state funerals, for door-knockers, beadles' staves and indeed anything fancied to be improved by a drooping black bow or bag. Crape was cheap and bought by the yard; it must have had the same effect on people that Do It Yourself always has – paint bought for one thing creeps all over the house – so that half a yard of crape left over went on one door-knocker, was quickly copied, and lo, by 1885, Grosjean in America was advertising his Funeral Annunciator, a tasteful method of draping the door of the house of mourning. 'In Cornwall the bird cages and indoor plants were put into black. In various parts of France all the domestic animals must be informed, crape must be attached to the pigsties and to the cat. Even the trees must be told and sometimes put into mourning.'[5]

There was even a tendency for widows, who always had the longest and deepest mourning, to stay in black for the rest of their lives, and all accessories would be to match, even the ear-trumpet. Full mourning was severe – two years in England. For the first year, unrelieved black, dresses trimmed with crape, 'all must be black; no shining materials – not even diamonds or pearls must be worn . . . For the following year the black may be relieved by white, grey, or coloured feathers, flowers, and ornaments.' Court mourning for the death of a sovereign was six months of unrelieved black, and the public was expected to wear black for six weeks. Black meant matt black – 'stuffs of a dull substance, suede cloth, crape cloth, frieze, serge, cashmere, crêpe-de-chine or nun's veiling. Neither satin nor velvet are admissible, nor ornaments of gold, diamonds or coloured jewels. Jet, of course, is the only mourning wear . . . The only mourning furs admissible are broad-tail, astrakhan, caracul, ermine, and chinchilla

Coachman's mourning cockade, pressed fibre. England, late nineteenth century

. . . Deep mourning must extend to servants. Neither coloured liveries nor cockades are allowed, and the rosettes at the horses' heads must be of black, the hammer-cloths of coaches are worked with black, and the footmen wear black plush breeches and black silk stockings with black buckles on their shoes . . . Gowns should be simply trimmed, and fall in long graceful folds, the effect of these in a soft, clinging stuff being remarkably beautiful. A statuesque and flowing appearance in drapery should be aimed at . . . Frippery is quite out of place . . .'[6]

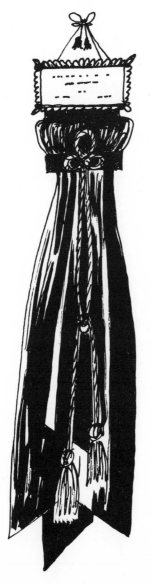

Above. Grosjean's Funeral Annunciator, and a funeral badge. United States, late nineteenth century

Right. The costume of a chief mourner at the time of Cook's third voyage, from a drawing by Webber. Tahiti, 1777–9

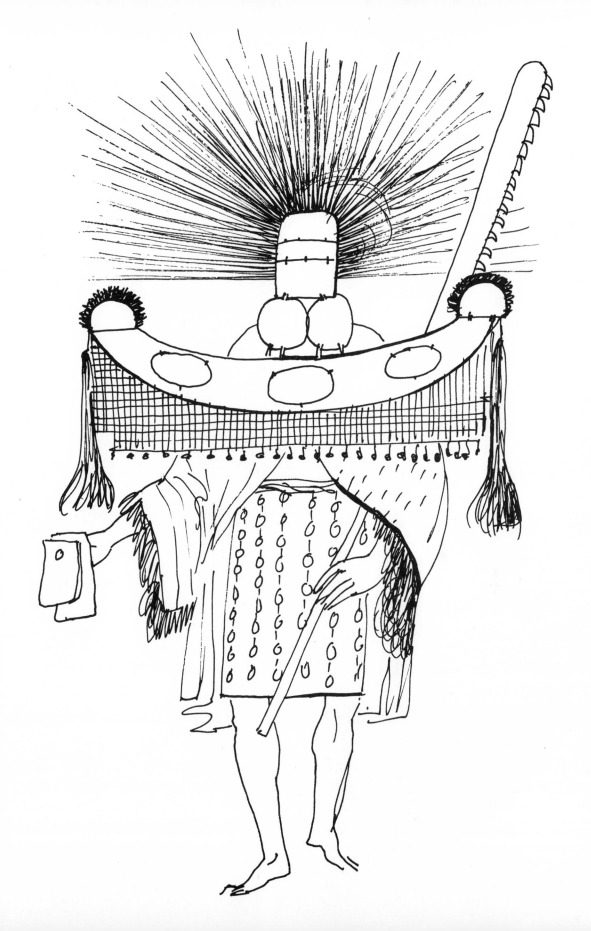

As late as 1925, it was possible for a book of etiquette for ladies to print the following rules: 'Widows usually wear mourning for two years, but lately the term has become much shorter. Crape is not much used except as a trimming, and this is left off after the first twelve months. The toque, or hat, and veil are worn for a year and a day, and white lawn collar and cuffs for the same period.

'With regard to jewellery, diamonds and pearls are frequently worn with very deep mourning, and they may quite properly be worn after a short period of mourning has elapsed. Gold is not usually worn until a year has passed.

'A widow is not expected to go into Society until at least three months have elapsed. Even then her visiting is confined to relatives and intimate friends. Gradually she reappears, though she should avoid dances and balls for at least a year.

'For children, daughters-in-law or sons-in-law, parents wear mourning for twelve months; ten months black, the last two months grey, white or mauve . . . For a brother, sister, brother-in-law or sister-in-law, the period of mourning varies from four to six months. After a month diamonds and pearls may be worn; gold a month later.' And on, on, through the ranks to first cousins, where all ends with the instruction, 'For a husband's relations, mourning periods are invariably the shorter ones'.[7]

Now it is all as if it had never been. In 1951 I wrote that 'special clothes for mourning have almost disappeared, except for a black band round the arm, or a curious little diamond of black cloth sewn on the coat-sleeve above the elbow, a miniature hatchment'.[8] I haven't seen either for years, and though the widows of heads of state still wear long veils of crape for state funerals, it seems unlikely that this fashion will last much longer.

Ear-trumpet for full mourning. England, nineteenth century

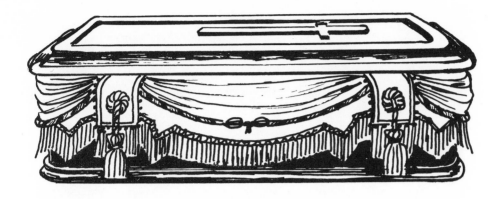

THE COFFIN

Everyone is in a coffin of flesh. After death, a wooden coffin may surround it, another step towards the ground.

Corpses are not always boxed. If it is believed that the corpse would pollute earth, fire or water, it will merely be wrapped up and exposed to the air until the flesh has decayed, when the bones may be gathered up and put in the earth or an ossuary. Most forms of water burial are simple, and for burning the corpse is usually wrapped in cloth, as in India. Earth is felt to offer most scope for elaboration; only in the United States has it reached the level of embalming the body and putting it in a steel casket for apparent preservation, and then using cremation to get rid of it quickly.

The photograph on page 72 shows the basic box in England today, the result of centuries of tradition, simple, spare, practical, one of the most beautiful things made by man. It is very difficult to get buried in this coffin as it stands; it will be tarted-up with mouldings, varnishes, polishes, and debased baroque handles before a corpse gets near it.

The earliest burials were simple, the body was put in a grave, lying on its back, or on its face, with feet towards Paradise, or with knees drawn up to the chin. Wrappings and boxes, and urns when pottery was

Left. A coffin in Burma (see page 91). *Above*. A. Freshl's Patent Drapes (see page 74)

Above. Rows of coffins in a London warehouse. In front of them are two unfinished ones, adult and child. Coffins are made in a range of stock sizes to fit all but abnormally tall or fat people. *Right*. The rubber sack

at a high level, came later. In Egypt, when the preservation of hot sand had given way to embalming, mummies were put in boxes which developed and multiplied through the dynasties until the mummy of a king would be buried in a nest of three wooden anthropomorphic coffins, the inner one very mummiform, closely built round the wrappings with a careful portrait mask, possibly in gold, over the face. Outside this was a larger, blunter case, still beautifully decorated, and outside this again a still heavier chest, keeping a little shape at the shoulders and feet and still carrying a portrait, but thickly painted with pitch, and sometimes enclosed yet again in a great sarcophagus for ultimate security. Very little security was achieved; tomb robbers often broke in in spite of rigorous precautions. The cases were jemmied open and the wrappings torn off in the search for jewels. Respectable archaeological tomb robbers have found most of the unrifled tombs by now, and the cases and corpses are popular exhibits in museums.

In China, social status laid down exactly what glories could be prepared; no sumptuary rules hindered the emperor but every level of officialdom had different privileges; for instance one rank of minister was restricted to an inner coffin four inches thick with an outer one of eight inches. These were usually fretfully carved from hardwood, and carved as early in life as possible, to be kept appreciatively in the house – what happened if, say, a district magistrate became a provincial governor and rated a thicker coffin?

The American Civil War is often said to have been the bloodiest war ever, and it was also full of firsts. First iron-clad, first scorched-earth, first war-guilt trials, first conscription, first modern embalming – all these can be disputed, but I think first rubber interment sacks must stand, elastic, deodorising, used at Gettysburg, weight 8 lbs 6 oz, used as sleeping bags in wet weather, as stretchers, and, inflated, as boats. In 1885, the rubber sack, like a long, flat bedsock with lacing round the ankle, was advertised

for civilian use, but it was decried by the undertakers as the 'iniquitous rubber sack' and the 'rubber sack abomination', and it never caught on.

It was elaboration that caught on, as we have seen with American embalming and shrouds. Mid-century coffins might be made of metal cast like drapery, or have black drapery hung round the sides. At first this was ruched up and nailed on by the undertaker, but later it came ready-made, like A. Freshl's beautiful patent drapes, gathered, fringed and finished with cord and tassels. Today, the climax of the American funeral is still the box. The basic coffin is a beautiful taut shape, narrowed at head and heels so that it can be manoeuvred easily up and down stairs, and here this shape has been lost in a great bodge. Not rectangular, because hardly any angles are visible at all, the thing is the oxidized metal offspring of a cumulus cloud and a half-sucked lozenge, and it is called a casket. All the forms are vulgar and coarse; debased classical, gothic, jazz, baroque, or nondescript. The finish is superb. Handles run right along the sides, supported by brackets in every style. Metal may be quilted, and there are caskets with angels, weepers, or the Last Supper *repoussé* along the front.

Below. Almond Fisk's Metallic, from the patent sketch. Unites States, 1848. During the nineteenth century, there were remarkable designs patented for everything; no less for coffins. An iron one was patented in England early in the century, and American patents describe mummiform, cruciform, tapered, rectangular, tear-drop coffins, made

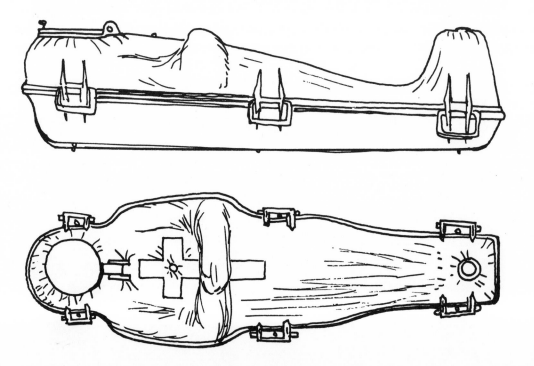

of metals, earthenware, glass, cement, papier-maché, rubber, and celluloid, while many continued to be made of wood covered with cloth, lined with satin and trimmed with silver in the manner of eighteenth century England. Metal steadily gained favour. About 1850–60, the casket, with straight instead of tapered shapes, was introduced, and lighter, more eternal, and more beautiful patterns were attempted. By the end of the century, the casket had almost won, and wood and metal were the usual materials, as now. *Below.* (*a*) Pre-casket. (*b*) High-art Metallic, probably Fisk, *c.* 1840. (*c*) Early casket. (*d*) First round-ended casket. All from an article in *The Sunnyside* for 1888 (see page 141) on Progress, leading up to (*e*) New! Magnificent Gothic Mahogany with endless Brass Handles

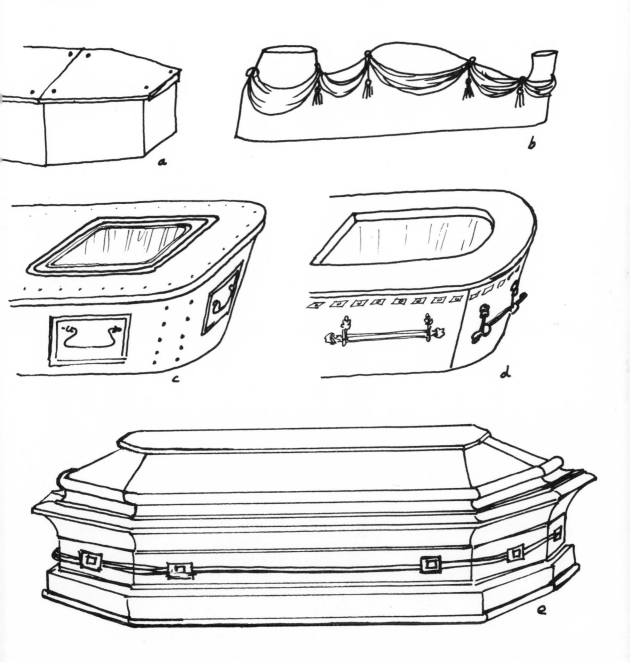

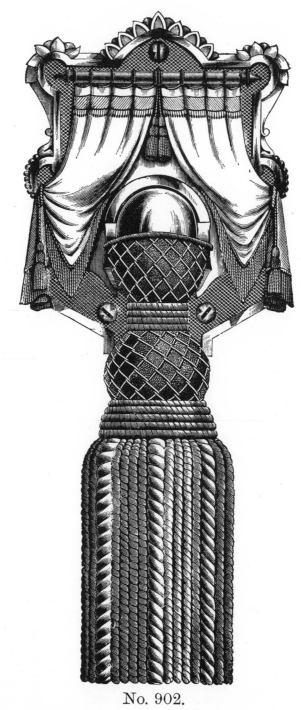

No. 902.

No. 905. Same Pattern one size smaller.

Above, right, and top of next page. Illustrations from a catalogue of coffin furniture.
United States, late nineteenth century[1]

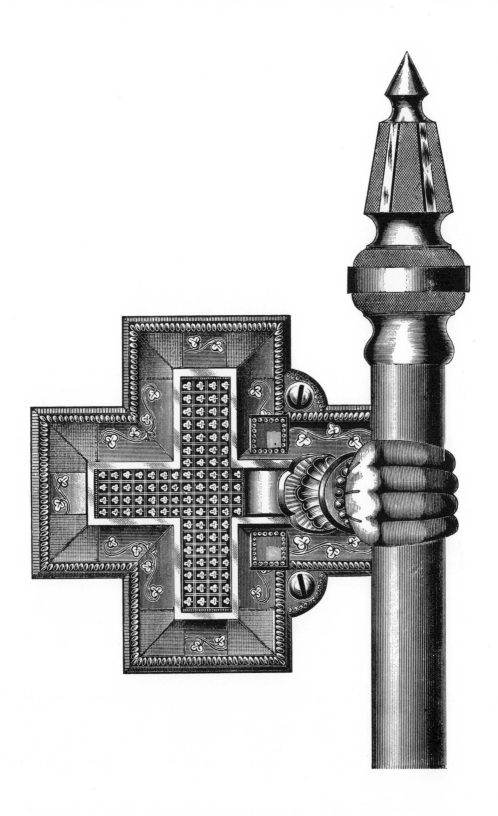

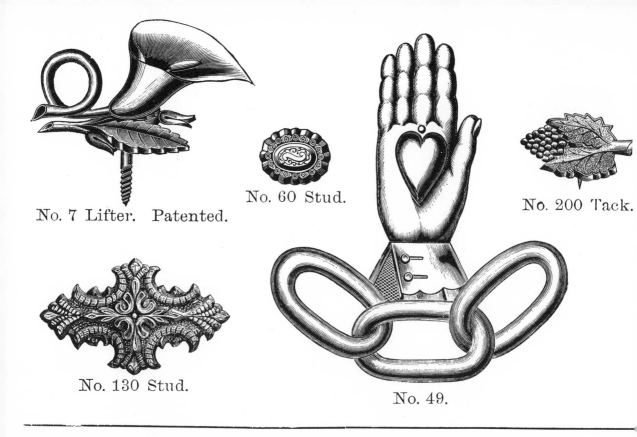

No. 7 Lifter. Patented.

No. 60 Stud.

No. 200 Tack.

No. 130 Stud.

No. 49.

PREPARED COFFIN SETS in Oak and Pitch Pin

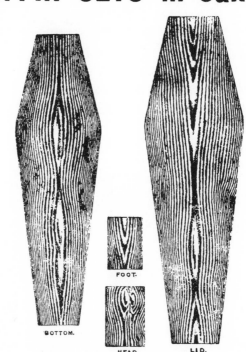

SIDES
KERFED FOR
BENDING.

LIDS SHAPED.

FINE
SAND PAPER
FINISH.

BOTTOMS IN
OAK, DEAL, or
PITCH PINE.

Any quantity
from One Set
upwards.

ALL JOIN
made by Invis
Jointing Mac

BOTTOMS
PLINTHS
Charged Ex

WOOD AL
thoroughly
STOVE DRI

FOR URGE
ORDERS, R
up our Priv
Telephone,
change No. 2
Nat., Hull

FOOT.

BOTTOM.

HEAD.

LID.

SIDE.

SIDE.

EACH SET : 1 Lid, 2 Sides, and 2 Ends.

LAVERACK & GODDARD, Ltd., Witham, HUL

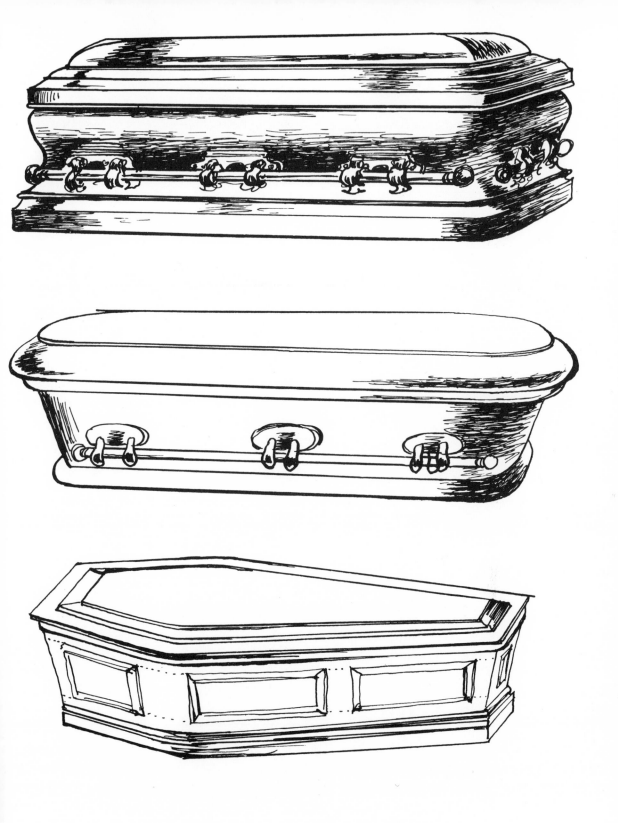

Lower left. Advertisement from 'The Undertakers Journal', England, 1910. *Above.* Two caskets, United States, and a coffin, England. All present day

79

At first glance, in spite of the occasional Last Supper, the caskets have a heavy family likeness, and it is surprising to learn that one manufacturer makes fifteen designs in cloth-covered wood for cremation, more than forty designs in nine different woods for cremation or burial, and another large range in 18–20 gauge steel or zinc for burial – though some people order a metal casket for cremation which is thrown away before burning. The woods are glorified with sturdy, pioneer names, and the metals are leafy, smoky, rose-taupey, and ethereally shaded. If the curved lid is lifted completely to show the whole corpse, this is 'full couch'; if the lid is made in two parts and only the left-hand side opened – 'half couch'. Sometimes the front hinges down as well. Inside, though, is the greatest glory, a cosmetic range of frosted crêpes and moon-dust velvets gathered, pleated, ruched and twitched into the most fantastic variety of linings, with a plump pillow, side-sheets, coverlet, and lid to match, pastels for ladies, ruby for gentlemen. A selection-room full of them looks like a shop-full of Victorian bassinets. Unfortunately, the old ladies who do the quilting are getting hard to replace, so that public demand for simpler interiors is being carefully fostered, and distinguished citizens are being steered to piping and plain padding. But the shapes are all so sleazy that the ruches look better.

Left. Repoussé angel on a casket. *Above.* Half-couch casket, covered with embossed cloth and lined with ruched velvet. Both United States, present day

81

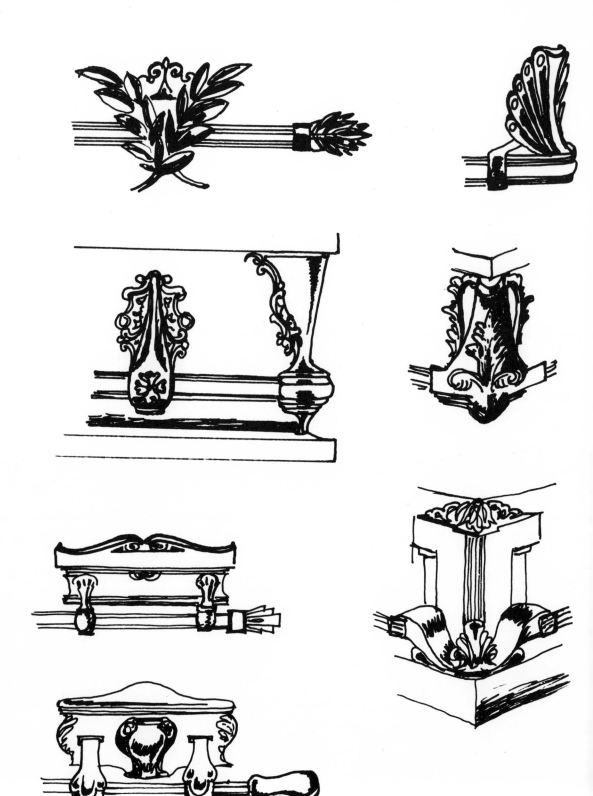

'shaded bronze' →

At Rest

Casket furniture. United States, present day

The wooden cremation caskets are elaborate, but the shapes are lost because the whole thing is covered with a broken-surfaced fabric like stamped velvet or crushed plush. Burning or burial, the poor eye boggles at the boxes.

The most elaborate caskets are for mausoleum burial. These are like the richest of the ordinary bronze or copper ones, but with a water-tight seal. A cellophane tag across one corner of the velvet says so, and the advertisements show white-coated scientists testing the seals with elaborate apparatus. A mausoleum casket has two lids, a single-section metal one on top of the usual divided one, which may in this case sometimes be made of glass. It is always the left-hand side of the casket that is open both in the showroom or over the corpse.

The corpse is now embalmed for eternal preservation, and sealed in a watertight steel casket. This in turn can be encapsuled in a custom-finished concrete burial vault, lined with pre-cast asphalt or fibreglass, warranty against earth-weight and underground elements. Very probably the whole heavy outfit will keep the body no longer than a sheet or a pine coffin: the light embalming used for a life-like appearance is very short-term indeed.

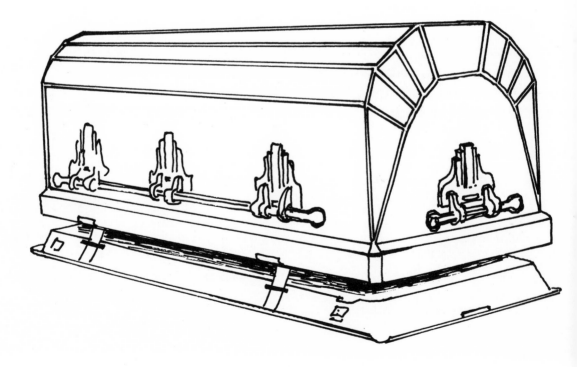

Metal burial vault to enclose the casket. United States, present day

In England, most people prefer coffins to caskets, and oak is the favourite material; 'a plain oak coffin'[2] has long been a cliché of superiority like 'an Englishman's home is his castle' and 'a good old tweed suit'. The change to flats and Carnaby Street clothes, though, does not indicate a switch to shiny plastic caskets – habitats and skins still interest us, but death does not. Two wars have obliterated our interest in funerals; people, said a tombstone maker, just don't want to know any more. Only interest makes big changes.

Meanwhile, tiny bored changes are taking place in the factories. Inflammable plastic coffin handles are used for cremation, and new variations of baroque and gothic are designed for them. Here and there a *cyma recta* changes to *cyma reversa*. For linings and coverings, rayon has joined calico, felt, velvet, plush, Domett, Silkette, Feltette, Louisine and Swansdown, and rayon and flannelette have replaced linen for shrouds. Regional differences still survive; brass fittings are favoured in the south of England, nickel in Wales and the north. Coffins are carried on the shoulders in the south, by the handles (which must therefore be tougher) in the north, and on the shoulders again in America and Ireland. Handles are made in many different designs; the bereaved very rarely make any choice, or even know that choice exists, so it must be the makers and the undertakers who like to choose.

In Scotland coffins have some extra features; the lining and frills more often match the shroud than in England, and may be more elaborately embellished. Silk courtesy cords with tassels are attached to the coffin, and certain invited mourners hold these while the coffin is lowered. A padded mattress matching the colour of the coffin is then lowered on more cords to cover the lid so that the sound of falling earth is muffled as the grave is filled in.

Coffins in Spain are a little different again, have flat lids and may have a brass cross and brass inlay and nails.

Coffins in Italy usually have a moulded lid, and sometimes brass decorations. Greek and Roman coffins were often made of stone, very deep, and standing on claw feet, and a sarcophagus is properly a stone coffin, but the name survives loosely for the shape, and they are sometimes seen, black and silver, for rich funerals today.

The simplest burials are those at sea. If there is a coffin at all, it is the merest box of planks. Often the body is sewn up in canvas, weighted, and slid into the sea.

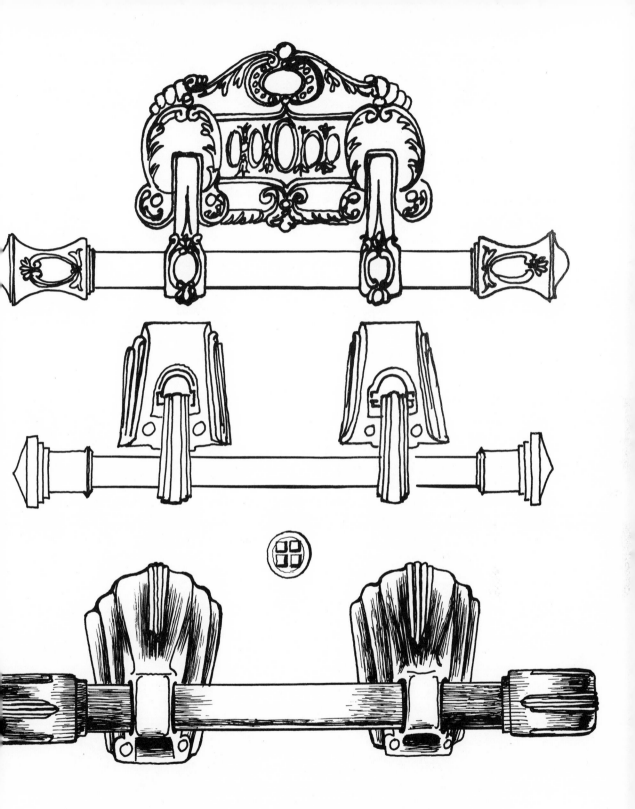

Coffin handles and nailheads. The rings, and the bottom handle on each page, are made of plastic for cremation. The top two on the right are viable handles used for carrying in the north; in the south, the coffin goes on the shoulders of the bearers. England, present day

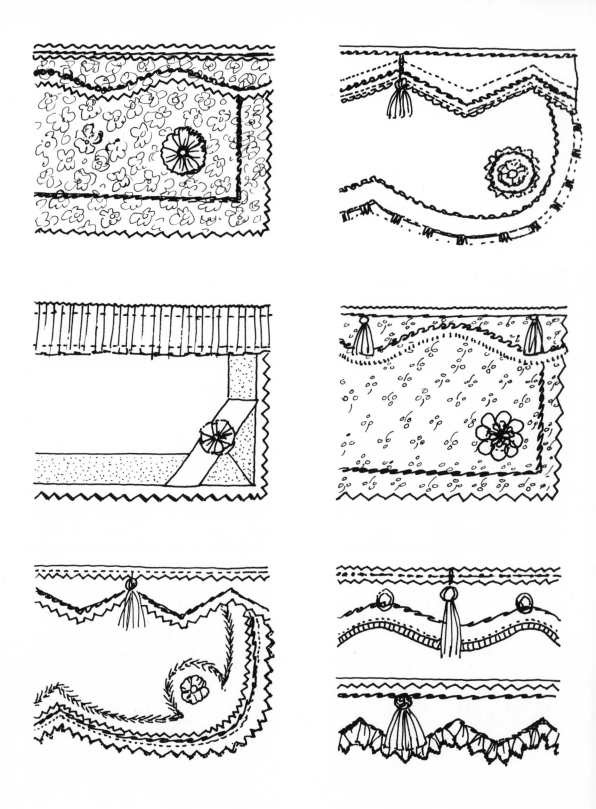

Coffin linings, rayon or cotton. England, present day

Above. Child's coffin covered in embossed white cotton fabric, decorated with white satin cross and silver braid. Similar coffins are made in black and gold for adults. *Below*. Coffin end, wood with stamped and gilded decoration. Both Portugal, present day

A fine quality coffin in mahogany and ebony with silver handles, on a display rack.
Portugal, present day. *Right.* The head of a Balinese coffin

In contrast are the coffins that the very rich or powerful sometimes order, golden, silver, crystalline, or jewelled. In the shape of yourself, in the shape of your lover – think of the most extreme fantasy, someone will have done it and is probably doing it today; gold-plated coffins are in enough demand to take their place in the catalogues.

But gold-plated coffins are dull besides the coffins of Bali, where corpses are burnt in carved animals. These accord with caste; half-elephant, half-fish for common man (so common that photographers always snap the others), a deer for a soldier, a winged lion for a king or a very holy priest, a cow for a noblewoman and a bull for a nobleman. They are made by specialist craftsmen from hollow trees with a lid in the back for the body. The carving is simple and the painting tough and free, fierce black eyes and sweeping horns. The animals are covered with cloth, perhaps bright velvet, and richly decorated with metal.

In Burma the beasts are bigger and better still. They are not coffins, but coffin-holders. Sometimes they are mounted on wheels and might be called hearses but the biggest ones stand still, and the corpse is brought to them in procession. They are made of papier-maché on strong wooden frames and for the funeral of a great man may be a hundred feet high. Elephants and tigers are the animals, sculptured with fire and observation, and brilliantly painted. The tigers hold the coffins in their snarls,

clasped between long white teeth, but the elephants, who could so easily take a coffin between tusks and trunk, bear the bodies in howdahs on their backs. There are effigies of men, too, towering dignitaries in their habit as they lived, with fierce eyes and sharp moustaches, papier-maché again but wearing real giant clothes and, if need be, outsize spectacles.

All these various boxes were made to take whole corpses, but there is a long history of separate burial or preservation of the heart in a smaller, often much richer, box; the Romans, for instance, used tiny urns inscribed COR. The fashion started again in the Middle Ages, probably because transport of a corpse back from the foreign wars was difficult. Certainly, a number of crusaders' hearts were sent home, and the custom was common enough for Ambrose Paré to say in his instructions for embalming that the heart should be taken out for the family to embalm and keep, and some people left instructions for their hearts to be sent to specially holy shrines. The little containers were made of gold, silver, enamel, crystal, ivory, fine woods, earthenware or lead, and might be decorated with carving or jewels. The hearts of the post-restoration Stuarts were

Above. Balinese coffins. *Right.* Anthropoid coffin, about 12 feet high, covered with imported red flannel, for the funeral of a chief. The corpse is put in through a hole in the back. French Congo, twentieth century

enclosed in silver covered with purple velvet, and the heart of Paul Whitehead, a poet, was kept in an urn in the Dashwood mausoleum at West Wycombe until it was stolen in 1839.[3] Heart burial continued as an occasional practise throughout the eighteenth century. I have been told of two hearts kept in a family vault in caskets resembling the coffins and standing at their feet. The heart boxes were lead-lined and filled with wheat-bran, like damp tea-leaves. In the one that was opened the heart was perfectly soft and fresh. The custom died out inexplicably in the nineteenth century with only one notable heart, Livingstone's in Africa.

Beaded calabash for storing the smaller bones of ancestors. Cameroons

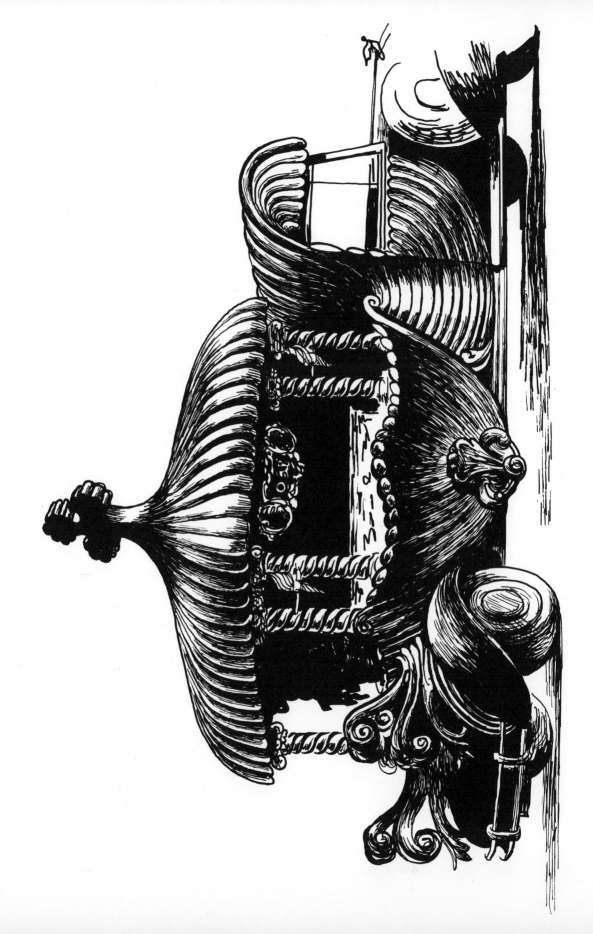

THE HEARSE AND THE UNDERTAKER'S SHOP

'Hearse' has changed its meaning. In the Middle Ages it was French (*herse*, a harrow), and was a triangular grid with spikes on the intersections to take candles. At first it was a simple piece of ironwork but later it became more elaborate and splendid, perhaps ornamented with brass. Extensions took drapery, fringes, flowers, poems, until the whole structure was large enough to surround the coffin with high gothic arches and railings. During the seventeenth and eighteenth centuries the hearses (by now, of course, baroque) became still more elaborate (especially in Italy) and were called catafalques or temples of honour, and sometimes hung from the roof of the church.

Many prints and drawings survive, but interpretation is hazardous. The lively skeletons carrying scythes, praying, prancing, crowned, were they real bones? Carvings? Painted on the flat? The enormous structures could have been on hire from the church, specials, projects, or fancy sketches to impress clients. Ogee curves above the coffin swing up to

Left. A carved wooden hearse. Buenos Aires, present day. *Above.* Embroidered initial for hearse, hangings, etc. Black velvet with silver. France, present day

97

great crowns, cherubs descend with drapery, and flames, cardinals, phoenixes, skulls, palms, ascend through the smoke of urns and torches to a pope on top. The candles tower in pyramids of little flames thirty or forty feet high.

Sometimes there are names and dates, and then we may assume that a drawing is the original design or was drawn from something real, or that an engraving will have been made so that prints could be given for mementos. Queen Mary II of England had four tall supporting obelisks, flags and candles; an Austrian royal catafalque of immense height was surmounted by five pyramids of candles, the central one supporting a life-sized crowned skeleton; a French water-colour of 1750 shows a black funeral chapel decorated with bat-winged skulls and tear-drops (a marginal pencil sketch shows a charming skeleton with drapery round its skull holding up a girandole); on an Italian print a skeleton points a bow and arrow at the congregation.[1]

Most of the decoration is impersonal, though one Italian artist is shown sitting under the baldachino at her easel; possibly a waxwork portrait.

By the seventeenth century, any prosperous townsman could hire elaborate mourning furnishings for the house, but the rich had them specially made. After the eighteenth century they became rare, their place being taken by special hearses for great occasions. The Shorter Oxford English Dictionary gives 1650 for the first use of hearse in this sense, and 1641 as for the first use of catafalque. Then confusion is heightened by a second definition, of catafalque as an open hearse (1855), but this fortunately did not gain favour.

Today the catafalque is still used in Roman Catholic countries, a framework holding up a black cloth or velvet baldachino and curtains trimmed with silver, matching the pall. Matching curtains with a fringed pelmet hang outside the church door, and there may be black and silver chair-covers for the mourners. Elaborately embroidered shields on the baldachino, pelmet and hearse take a series of interchangeable letters, so that the initial of the deceased's surname may be displayed. For a cheaper funeral, the draperies will be less elaborate. For the cheapest, there will be only a pall over the coffin.

Sometimes a corpse has to be moved to another town or country for burial and the coffin will then be moved by van, train, plane or ship, conforming to various regulations, but quite simply; elaborate transport is normally used only for the actual funeral.

Apart from burial at sea, where the ship is incidental, ships are now used for funerals in the western world only for the transport of the corpse as freight, but in the past they have been an integral part of the funeral of a ruler in various cultures, sometimes being used as a coffin or a tomb when the body was put on board with treasures, slaves, food, chariots – whatever grave-goods were held desirable at the time – and the whole thing was buried. Sometimes, though, the ship has been both hearse and pyre, towed out to sea and left in flames to drift with the wind and tide, surely the most splendidly wasteful and impressive of all funerals.

One kind of water funeral survives in Europe; in Venice the hearses are gondolas, trimmed with black fringe and silver, and therefore richer than the ordinary ones in the true hearse manner. There is a catafalque-cabin, but the coffin stands out in the open under flowers and an acolyte holds a big cross in front.

The Gipsies used to burn the bodies of their kings and queens with all their possessions in their living-vans. By-laws everywhere now prevent all private burials or burnings, but nevertheless the van and possessions may still be burnt, wasteful and impressive again.

Some of the most interesting hearses were those made in Europe and America during the nineteenth century. We shall look at the enormous tributes called funeral cars with the processions they were part of; here are the kind hired out for ordinary funerals, with panels and hangings showing armorial bearings or professional interests added if required.

In the early part of the nineteenth century in England, hearses were general in the towns, with simple classical-revival designs, heavy drapery and open sides. Then came the Gothic Revival, which engulfed most ecclesiastical design completely, and might have been expected to change the design of hearses, but no; hearses quickly returned to the richest possible source and remained obstinately baroque, the Lord Mayor's coach at last for those who walked in life. A good gothic hearse is preserved at Shrewsbury, though, with solid sides, carved balls as an economical substitute for ostrich plumes, hammer-cloth, and roof, all wood, with heavy carved decoration picked out with a little gold.

The baroque hearses varied in intensity, subdued for high-class funerals in London and New York and very richly carved in the Southern States and in Europe. Most of them were crowned with plumes, an almost universal sign of rank, whether they were deserved or not. Open sides were out of fashion by the middle of the century, being replaced by drapery or wooden panels carved to represent it, and later by glass, plain, bevelled, or magnificently engraved in the pub-and-front-door tradition. Sometimes the roof was held up on columns and the sides just glazed, sometimes the whole body was oval or even had returning curves and glass to fit. Hearse-building was a specialist trade and the newest designs were advertised to the undertakers.

Perfection was expected. Black horses were bred in Belgium for the funeral trade; sometimes they were rusty and had to be dyed blacker; the hooves were always blacked. If the tails were short or skimpy, flowing false ones were strapped round the real tail, growing out of a crupper filled in with a little piece of hairy hide. Caparisons of black velvet drapery hung down the horses' sides, and could cover the necks if the manes were thin. The harness was black trimmed with silver, and until this became illegal just before World War I, bunches of black ostrich plumes stood up between the horses' ears. Four or six horses drew a hearse, six needing an outrider on the near leader.

Mute, and undertaker's man carrying a feather tray (see pages 167 and 168), and hearse. England, 1826

carrying the feathers

Many undertakers kept small white hearses for children's funerals, and occasionally adults have had white hearses, too. Father Damien was buried with great chic in Belgium, in a completely enclosed white hearse with black plumes, drawn by white horses, also with black plumes. White hearses, baroque or bus-like, smothered in palm-leaves and flowers, have also been very fashionable in Italy.

Well-off mourners followed the hearse in their own carriages, and the great might send an empty carriage (identified by the crest on the door-panels) to the funeral of a social inferior who was yet deemed worthy of more attention than a wreath. The carriage horses of the immediate family were put into mourning for the necessary months; the bright patent-leather, braid or beaded headbands were taken from the bridles and replaced with black ones made of woollen, braid or satin ribbon according to class. Matching rosettes of great beauty and complexity went under the ears (horse millinery was another specialist trade). The coachman and footmen wore black cockades, and great houses kept black hammer-cloths in store.

Left. Funeral horse's satin ear-rosette and false tail. *Above*. Nineteenth century hearses see note[2]

Above. Hearse, carved wood painted black and silver with glazed sides. England, late nineteenth century.[3] *Left*. Hearse; carved and gilded wood. Portugal, mid-nineteenth century (from a trade catalogue)

The end came quite quickly, with the motor car; undertakers were as quick to see its advantages as everyone else. Steam transport had been used in many fields (such as roundabouts, ships, and trains) to increase weight and richness to the limit, but the internal-combustion engine came when simplicity was becoming fashionable, and, by the time motors were powerful enough to take heavy coachwork, taste in England and the United States was swinging away from plumes and crape so that the motor hearse soon developed soberly on private-car lines. Today it is like a large black estate wagon without any wood.

Only in countries where baroque hearses had been really extravagant did they retain their vigour for the motors. In Portugal it had been the custom of the undertakers to buy up the coaches of noble families who were too fashionable to keep old ones or had become too poor to keep them at all. These coaches had been made in Paris, Rome or Lisbon in the most sumptuous baroque styles and the undertakers painted the decorated panels black, but left the carved decoration with its original gilding. They became very ingenious at adapting even small carriages for cheaper funerals, replacing the coachman's seat with a carrier to hold the coffin across the width of the chassis, where it was of course covered with a richly embroidered pall. Other small carriages, with the decoration changed in the same way, were used to carry the priest, who followed the coffin. This carved and gilded decoration went onto the first motor hearses and continues today for working-class funerals. The hearses and the priests' cars are made to match and are very pretty indeed. Richer people have international-style hearses without a scrap of decoration on them, and undoubtedly the baroque carving will not survive for long; already some of it has a perfunctory look.[4]

The motor was not the only form of mechanised transport to replace the horse for funerals; in several cities in America where the railway line passed near the main cemetery, special hearse coaches were built which could take the corpse and mourners behind a crape-draped engine.

1910 was a key year for funeral innovations. Mr John White, aged seventy-seven, dying at 5 Tin Street, Cardiff, asked that one of his son's traction engines should be used for a hearse. So the 'General White' was nicely draped, with wreaths of white flowers round the axles and a huge flower harp on the front surmounted by Prince of Wales feathers, and the procession went down Queen Street. In Cleveland, Ohio, an automobile funeral car was built to seat thirty-six people, with room for the casket and flowers. It replaced nine mourning coaches, could be driven right up to the grave, and used as a chapel on a wet day. In Burma, trolley cars came into use to carry the coffin and catafalque, all most exquisitely made, and in Mandalay only the year before a white pasteboard elephant almost one hundred feet high had been made for a royal funeral. It was mounted on wheels and the coffin was hauled onto its back with cables. Probably it was the largest recorded hearse. In England, the Undertaker's Journal had an article on the motor hearse, with three examples. All three carried the coffin low and enclosed while the driver was exposed to the weather. Mr Pargetter's was glass-sided with a railing on top round the roof and a hammer-cloth, a small traditional hearse sitting on a motor chassis. Mr Thompson's, a 12 hp Wolseley, was a pioneer piece of simple design, and the last picture shows Messrs Stevens and Bean's Automorguemobile from Fresno, California. (On the next page we are back

Automorguemobile . Driver sits *beside* corpse

in the nineteenth century with a wood-engraving of a bearded man in a carpenter's paper hat varnishing a carriage while a balloon comes out of his mouth, 'THE FISH AND RING BRAND IS THE BEST'.)[5]

Between the wars, the motor steadily superseded the horse, so that today the horses would have to be brought in by train for a horse funeral in London – though such a funeral was seen in Croydon in 1945, led by a mute with crape round his top hat walking before the horses. In the nineteen-twenties the fine workmanship of the carriage tradition still held in beautifully draped windows with fringes and tassels and, as late as 1938, Messrs Sayers and Scoril in America had a fine carved car with rich drapes; 'shows the trend'. But they were wrong; in both England

"shows the trend"

and the United States the trend was for large glossy black Rolls Royce, Daimler, and Cadillac hearses with nothing special about them except the rollers. These are still the trend in England though black is losing ground, and design in America is now racier, so the hearse is likely to be grey or rose-beige with stiffly-folded drapery to tone. Often they are sham convertibles with sham springs, but the following cars will probably be black with the mourners in black spectacles.

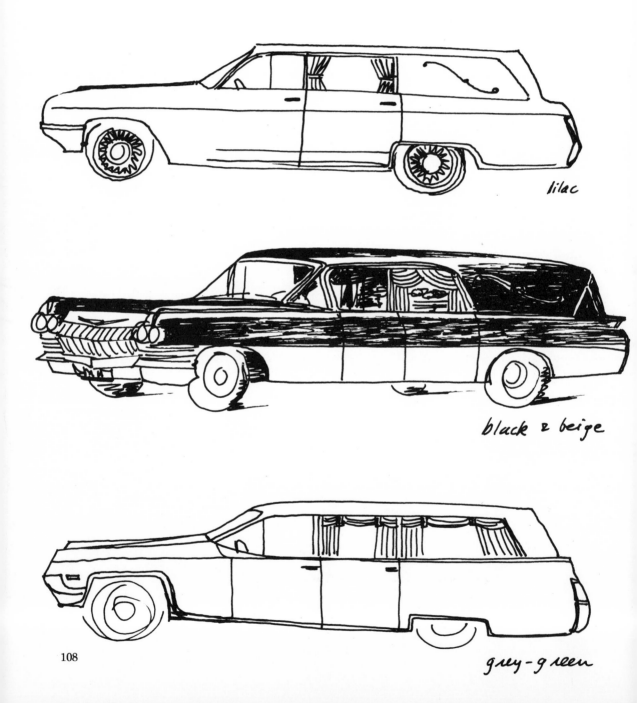

lilac

black z beige

grey-green

With next page, motor hearses decorated with carved and gilded wood. Portugal, present day

In both countries the shroud, coffin, flowers, printing, and tomb are all bought outright, but the hearse and attendants are hired from the undertaker, who emerged as a specialist in England about three hundred years ago.

Primitive funerals were carried out by the family and friends with priests for prayers or ritual, and small remote communities even today may rely on the local carpenter for coffins; but once an elaborate death ritual is evolved, the specialists evolve with it. We know that in Egypt there were funeral trades of dissectors, apothecaries, surgeons, priests, painters, carpenters and masons, but there were probably other specialists as well – weavers of the hundreds of yards of fine linen bandages, for instance.

In Rome, there were professional criers and mourners, and for the first time the funeral director appears. The early Christians despised the Romans' elaborate pyres and prayers, and persecution made ostentatious funerals impossible, but even when persecution was over and catacombs were unnecessary, simplicity remained fashionable (except as usual for the funerals of the great) right through the Middle Ages, when even the promotion of funeral clubs did little towards elaboration.

The Renaissance revived Roman ideas of splendour for the rich. At first everything was managed with the estate carpenters, but gradually the black hangings for rooms, churches and beds (even the bed-clothes were black), special painting for coaches and caparisons for horses, as well as the clothes and gloves and jewellery for mourners, all became unmanageable and cripplingly expensive, so that by the end of the seventeenth century undertakings, as we know it, was an established trade in England with all the drapery for hire.[6]

The undertaker advertised with engraved cards[7] and painted sign-boards. The shop-fronts were black, lettered and picked out with gold and silver, and it became the thing to have a coffin in the window, richly decorated with brass-headed nails in bands and crosses. Later, when the number of coffin designs multiplied beyond mere differences of nails and woods, model coffins were made to display in the shop and to take to the houses of the richer customers.

At the same time the violent symbols of death were replaced by black edges on the cards and bill-heads, the explicit hanging signs went, and marble angels and immortelles, instead of coffins, went into the window.

After World War I, a lot of these Victorian shops were re-decorated in muted Georgian style, grey instead of black, with tasteful lettering, subdued Adam waiting-rooms, and an ecclesiastical-type grey curtain suspended on bands of fabric at the back of the window; in front, a cremation urn or casket, looking as like a vase or a presentation as possible. Today, the undertakers' shops are following the sad descent of

WILLIAM
BECKETT
FUNERALS ARRANGED
THE BRITISH ISLES &
WILLIAM SWAN
FUNERAL FURNISHER
55
WENLOCK

all shops into uniformity, and may have coloured mosaic fascias, bare wood, plastic lettering and a striped blind just like the hairdressers' next door. In the older towns in both England and the United States the doctor, architect, lawyer, estate agent and antique dealer usually own all the nicest eighteenth-century houses on the main street; in America, the funeral director will probably have joined them, or, if there were no gracious residences available, will have built between the wars premises as like a house as possible, though there will be garaging, interview-rooms, embalming rooms, storage rooms and at least one large rest-room behind the private façade. In small communities, the funeral parlour may be a wooden shack among other shacks, distinguished by a painted sign, RELIABLE UNDERTAKING, while in the cities, the big shops will look not so much like houses as like churches and be further sanctified by a vaguely ecclesiastic name. In both countries, contemporary architecture is beginning to be accepted.

In France, the shops tend to black vitriolite, and POMPES FUNEBRES, white or silver, is written in the sans-serif or *arts decoratifs* letters of the nineteen thirties. Most of them have open backs to the windows, which are full of immortelles, though the bead-and-wire flowers which held their own through the thirties have now given way to plastic and highly glazed china. Continental undertakers need plenty of storage space, because the custom of draping the church doors, which may be enormous, is still kept up. There will be a pelmet and curtains made of black velvet embroidered and fringed with silver, and a shield with the surname initial of the dead may be mounted at the top, as on the hearse, and on the matching velvet pall over the coffin in the chancel or chapel, and on the chairs round it for the mourners.

An undertaker setting up in a small town in England today will look for a site with two completely separate entrances, one at the back or side for hearses and stores and the other (flanked for choice by quiet and dignified shops) in a central street. This is for the customer, who goes into a reception area and then into an interview room. There will also be an office, one or two 'chapels of rest' where the dead may be visited, an embalming room, stores, and garages. In a city, there will be more interview rooms, chapels of rest and offices, plus mourners' rooms, a coffin show-room, and a flower room.

The undertaker's shop will be as central as possible so that the name becomes familiar to a lot of people, but the monumental mason's yard is

Undertakers' shops in North London. Nineteenth century, surviving

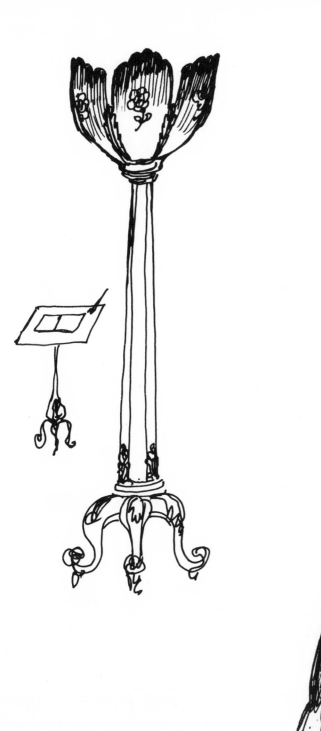

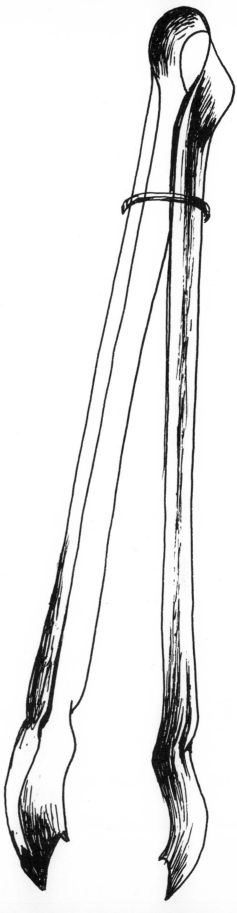

Left. The regalia of Les Frères de la Charité, an undertakers' benevolent society founded in 1240. France, mid-nineteenth century. *Above.* Red glass lamp and register stand. *Right.* Food tongs, undertaker's goodwill-builder. United States, present day

usually near the cemetery. Originally, of course, this was to minimize transport of the heavy stones; motors and small monuments have changed this, but it is still good for trade to have the yard placed so that the mourners will see it as they leave the cemetery, and sometimes there is a florist's shop or stall there too.

The mourners may meet at the house or the undertaker's, or go straight to the cemetery or crematorium, according to fashion or religion, class or area, and so the size and splendour of the undertaker's chapel will vary with local custom, but his whole establishment will always aim at a cosy, reassuring domesticity. It is, alas, impossible for him to make it homey for us all with all our different ideas about home, so he aims either at the comfortable middle of the middle classes with reproduction furniture, fitted carpets, harmless chairs, knole sofas, pelmets, and flowers, or, if most of his trade is working class and he is going in for a mosaic fascia, contemporary with canted legs. Either way, you wouldn't know where you are. A professional anonymity has settled on the place and the undertaker prefers to be called funeral director, as if a funeral were a film.

The undertaker and his staff used to wear heavy black with top hats and, for the funeral, sashes and hat-bands of crape. Today, even the mourning coat and striped trousers are going out of fashion, and black is being replaced by dark grey; throughout the whole procedure of funerals in England, grief should not be shown, and everything is organized to cushion sensibility. Opinion on this is divided; one school holds that life is easier if you never crack, the other that it would be better for us if we did. Most people rub along making as little fuss as possible and getting back to normal as quickly as they can.

Recommendation, family habit, small ads in local papers, and a familiar name are felt to account for enough trade in England; in the United States promotion is extensive, and may include spots on the local TV networks. Every visitor to the funeral home will probably be given a good-will builder – diary, shopping-list, mending kit, palm-leaf fan, aspirin-carrier or such small object with the name and telephone number as a constant reminder – 'Show Helpfulness and your Name on the Lid'. New residents in a district are usually greeted by the welcome wagon; it brings samples and gifts from local traders and there will be something handy from the funeral home among them.

Undertaker selling pre-need. United States, present day

Finis

THE FLORAL TRIBUTES

Hair, blood, flowers, bread, wine, meat, earth, honey, jewels, animals, men, women and simulacra have all at different times been put onto or into graves to help the dead or to lay the ghost. The expensive, messy or murderous offerings have mostly gone, though in some countries, like Mexico, graves are planted with what you will – electric lamps, shells, toys, vases, wine-glasses, plaster dogs, medicine bottles and film spools – anything to make it more like home – and as noble a set of symbols can be invented for this second list as for the first, arming the dead man as it does with illumination, protection, entertainment, spiritual and physical refreshment, company, health, and the means of communication.

Until quite recently flowers made very suitable offerings, easily available, often free, light to carry, widely regarded as symbolic of the shortness of life and very heartening in sorrow if looked at with enough concentration.

Flowers appear in ancient paintings and carvings of funerals, usually woven into garlands or scattered. In Europe the custom seems to have declined after the Middle Ages and certainly in the eighteenth century the mournful evergreens of cypress, yew and laurel were much more fashionable than flowers. Then the nineteenth century came up trumps

Left. A lyre with broken strings. United States, early twentieth century. *Above.* Angling club tribute (see page 128). England, present day

a

b

Mother

c

d

Left. (a, b and c). Three tributes from America; 1865, 1877, and present day (plastic).
(*d*) Germany, 1951. *Above.* The Golden Gates Ajar, latest conception of Mr Le Moult of
the Bowery. United States, 1885[1]

with what were probably the most splendid tributes of all. (It is impossible to be sure – flowers are ephemeral, and records vary in completeness. We *can* feel sure that if the Ancient Egyptians had had elaborate flower-works, these would show up somewhere on a wall or a scroll, but we cannot feel sure about Easter Island or Ankor.)

In the late nineteenth century, and still occasionally today, flowers for graves were less used to show the beauty of the flowers themselves in tribute than as a medium for artistic expression, and every florist was expert in wiring, dyeing, and turning flowers inside out and every which-way to make pearly gates, empty chairs, broken harps, cushions, books, hearts, wings, anchors and lyres, as well as the dead level of crosses and wreaths.

The flowers for the funeral of Queen Victoria are said to have cost £80,000 . . . 'The mass of floral tributes was of unprecedented beauty. Some of them astonished by their magnitude. The Queen Regent of Spain sent a wreath seven feet high; the business firms of Queen Victoria Street presented a Royal Standard five feet by nine composed entirely of violets, geraniums and mimosa. Australia's large wreath was of finest orchids, while the King's Scholars of Westminster offered a wreath of pink and white flowers measuring twelve feet. The immense shield of the 7th Hussars, composed of 60,000 dark Russian violets, bore the monogram and title of the regiment and the Queen's crown, worked in golden narcissi, and looked very beautiful. The 9th Lancers' shield of white azaleas and lilies of the valley, with crossed lances formed of mignonette, crimson carnations, and white flowers, pleased much by its originality and taste.

'Some of the private tributes showed tender care and thought. People gave as much as a hundred pounds for a wreath, and nearly everyone remembered that lilies of the valley were the Queen's favourite flower . . . The King of Portugal's tribute was a crown of lilies, white orchids and violets; the Tsar and Tsarina's a wreath of Parma violets and mauve lilac tied with black and yellow ribbons, the national colours . . . the Duke of Hamilton had his crest, a bleeding heart surmounted by a crown, worked in red and white flowers. Other tributes in the shape of Victoria Crosses, crosses, wreaths of laurel and palm, cushions, and anchors of flowers, harps with broken strings, shields, etc, made up a rare and marvellous collection.'[2]

Two wire frames for crosses, and a tin cross to take flowering bulbs on the grave. England, twentieth century

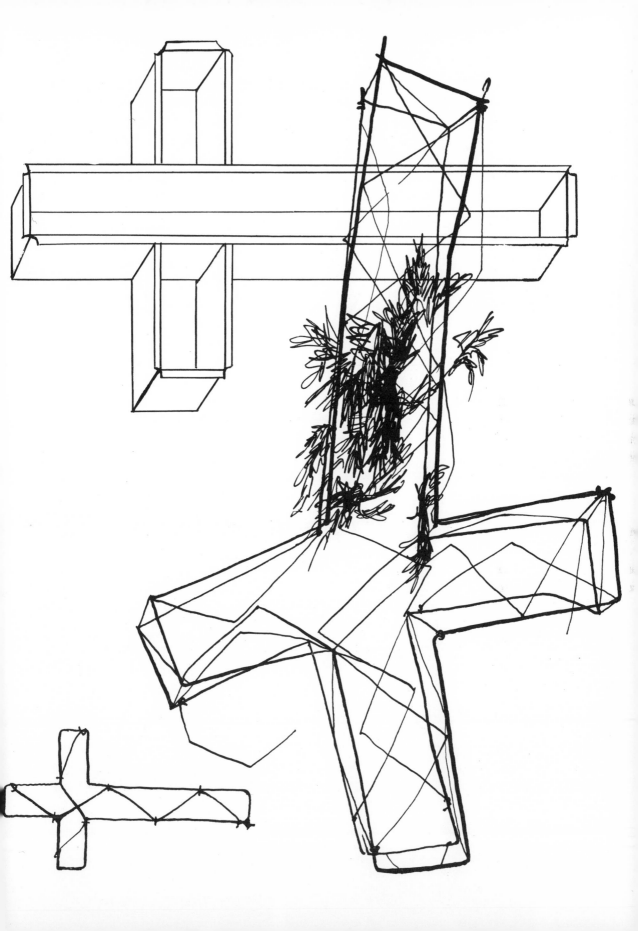

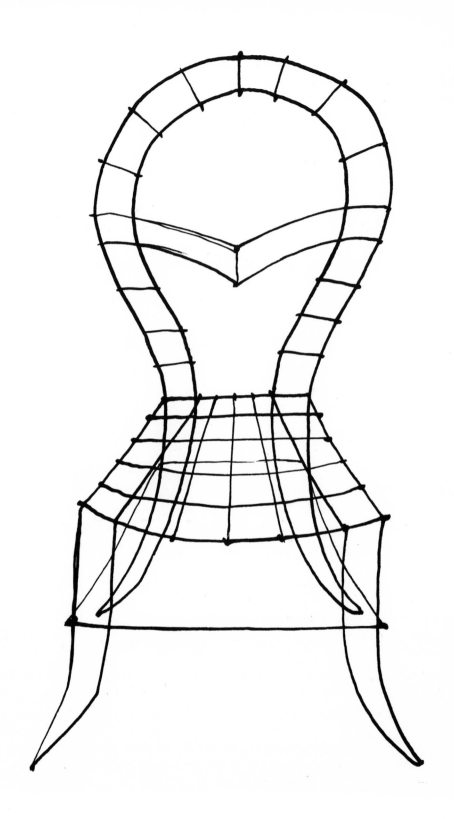

Big florists, or the shops near the cemetery gates, held beautiful ready-made wire frames of most of these in stock and would always make or order regimental or family crests, portraits, or indeed, almost anything anyone fancied. The frame was packed round with moss, wired in place and kept damp, and then a background (perhaps evergreen or everlasting flowers or daisies) was put on over the moss, each little bit being twisted onto a wire, stuck in, and turned at the end to hold fast. Then the flowers and maidenhair fern were added, loose for an artistic, free-thinking wreath, tighter for a conventional one or a cross, and very tight for the representational effects. To help recognition, it was usual to stick gilt letters on wire or ribbon proclaiming THE EVER-OPEN GATE or GRANDPA'S CHAIR. These letters are more used today to give prominence to the senders' name; FROM NEIGHBOURS, FROM COLLEAGUES IN THE OFFICE, FROM ALL AT THIRTEEN – and I once saw a hearse with two huge tributes fastened up on the roof, a wreath FROM LOVING WIFE and a harp FROM BELOVED MOTHER. Game, set, and match.

Flowers can be in season with simplicity as reason or excuse, or exotic for opulence or a last gesture, or funereal for symbolism, with violets and lilies in first place, and the scale still runs from a bunch of wild flowers to the blanket of orchids essential to the funerals of famous film stars and gangsters. These, with great jazz musicians, have legendary funerals, but the flowers on investigation have always been lavish rather than interesting – like the orchid blanket. There have been one or two floral movie-cameras, though.

Carnations, tough, stiff, and available all through the year, are the florists' standby, with daffs in spring, roses and gladdys in summer, chrysanths in autumn, and hot-house lilies as high spots. All these are still made into wreaths, and occasionally crosses, but today's smart thing is the sheaf, a flat, backless bunch, short stems at the bottom, long stems at the top, or so you think till you try to send them to a hospital after the funeral, when the undertaker will show you how the long stems are only wire and the whole thing really heads only and useless. The sheaf is delivered in cellophane, an abominable condom probably tied with purple cellophane ribbon. It is nobody's job to take this off, so there they all lie wilting on the grave, rain outside, condensation in, the most disgusting mess in the world.

Nevertheless, the true tribute persists, and not only can Pearly Gates and Empty Chairs still be seen, but football coupons made of flowers are

Wire frame for The Empty Chair. England, twentieth century. The same theme also occurred at the funerals of Ashanti chiefs, where the dead man's stool was prominent in the ritual

Words for tributes. *Top*. Metal, letters clipped on. England, present day. *Centre*. Gilt letters on silk ribbon. France, present day. *Bottom*. Gilt metallised plastic. United States, present day

Words for tributes. *Top.* Mauve plastic. England, present day. *Centre.* As top left. *Bottom.*
Here the whole tribute spells the name of the dead. England, present day

now fashionable, and on the afternoon of October 22nd, 1965, the City of London Cemetery and Crematorium could show a beautiful piano four feet long made of white chrysanthemums outlined with pink ones. The keyboard was scarlet carnations and the pedals and sharps were silver paper. In silver on a purple ribbon: GOOD NIGHT POP. On a card: In Loving Memory of Dear Dad. On a sheet of writing paper:

> *Around a Piano we have*
> *Gathered through the Years*
> *A Legacy of Happiness and*
> *Laughter that Shines*
> *Through our tears.*

For another cremation, on the same afternoon, DAD, eighteen inches high in white chrysanths on gold wire. For another, an angling club sent a fish three feet long made of white carnations. The eye was a November 11th poppy, and red carnations and roses were used to write HERS along the flank. The mouth was red roses, and the whole fish was outlined with pink carnations, red roses, and loops of pink ribbon. For another, a coffin-shaped wreath four feet long, exquisitely made of orchids, roses and carnations. Do not let the sheafs depress you – some people still know how it should be done.

Feather bird, white or pastel-coloured, mounted on wire to perch above the flowers. England, present day

Porcelain immortelle with perching dove and dark green tin leaves. Sometimes the hands appear instead of the dove. England, late nineteenth century

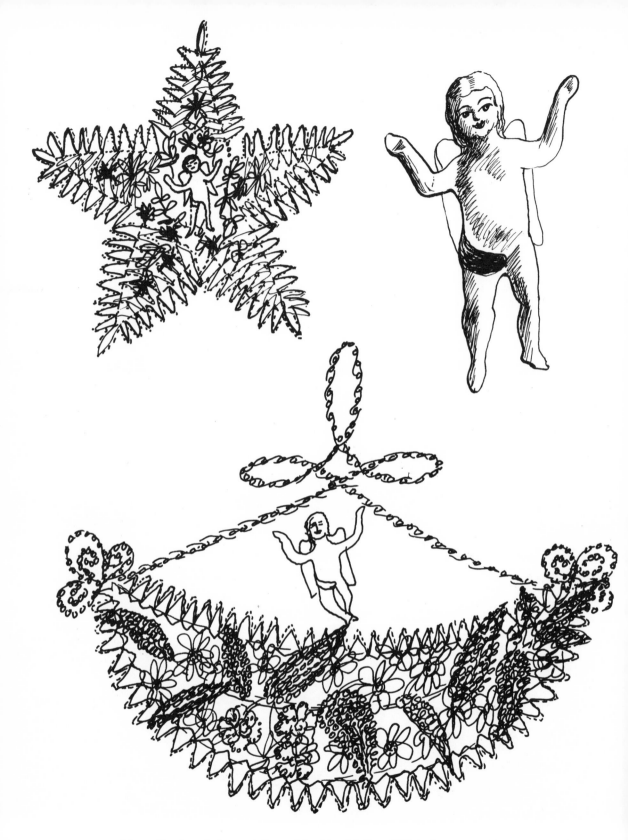

Above. Beadwork immortelles with cherubs for children's graves. France, twentieth century. *Right.* (*a*) Living ivy cross. England. (*b*) Metal No. 2 Century Plant, twelve leaves. United States, late nineteenth century. (*c*) Chinese paper flower wreaths, present day

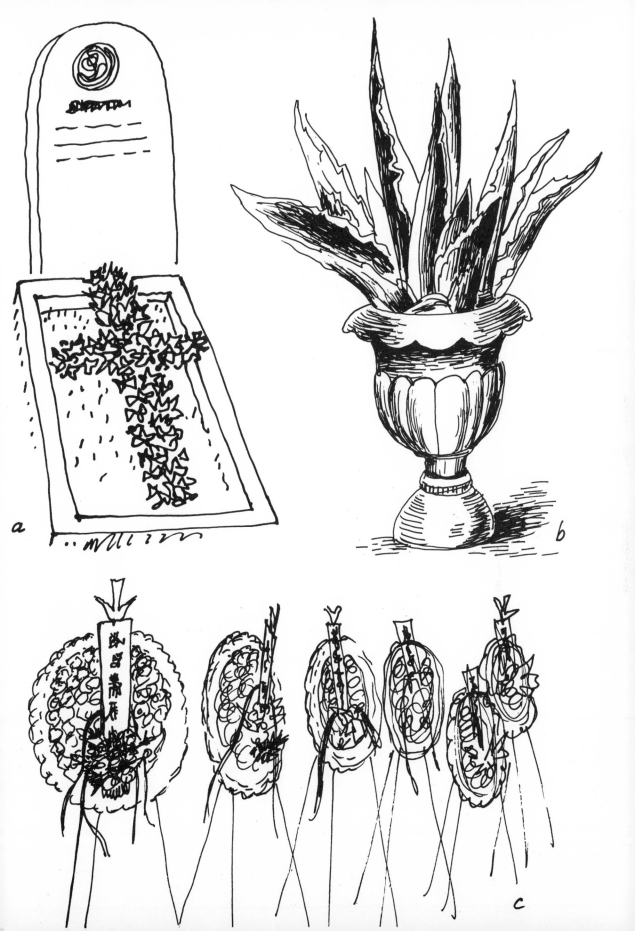

a

b

c

Tributes are only for the funeral, and after that, though sheafs may be coarsely taken to the grave at any time, its continued embellishment is with ordinary bunches of flowers put in water in jampots, or in enamelled tin, or fibreglass, or china in the shapes of urns, cornets, or vases. Easier maintenance is achieved with grass, marble chips, planting-out shrubs, or immortelles. We shall consider the containers and the chips later but the immortelles stand for flowers and are for this chapter.

Immortelles were the first labour-saving devices used on tombs, and the early ones were extraordinarily beautiful. In England they were mostly white, made of porcelain or tin, carefully modelled copies of roses, lilies, daisies, carnations and a special little trumpet-shaped flower for filling in gaps – the makers had their own specialities. There were buds, leaves (sometimes green), doves to perch on top, and an occasional pale pink or yellow flower for variety. They were made by hand, the petals gathered on wires so that they could be fastened onto a stout wire frame just as the florist wired live flowers on to frames, only the immortelles needed no moss. Wreaths were the usual thing, but there were crosses, harps, chairs, hearts as well, and a glass dome (or a heart- or harp-shaped glass case) on a tin base could be bought to preserve them. Later, wire cages covered the glass to preserve *that*, and with dirt and condensation and wire, the pretty wreaths soon became invisible. Plastic flowers have replaced them today – easier to clean as they can be dunked in a bucket of detergent and come up just like new. The colours are at least as bright as life, and there are good evergreens and ears of corn. Plastic wreaths are so popular in America that they are part of the stock of supermarkets.

In France, much larger immortelles are still made of small glass beads threaded on wire and bent into sharp loops for petals and leaves. A shaded effect is often worked outwards from the centre of the petal. The flowers are necessarily less realistic than the porcelain ones; some pretty ones are simply fans of round loops that do not pretend to representation at all. Colours are funereal, black, white, grey, and mauve, and the trophies are often very large, and held up on iron tripods and easels. They used to be put in deep box-frames with metal-crochet edges, or under glass houses on the graves. They are always gloomy and spidery except for the small white trophies made for children.

The bead-work is still made, but is being replaced in the hearts of the French by highly glazed china posies, crosses, wreaths. Clumsy and inelegant, dull crimson roses, thick green leaves. They are a step back into the barbola-world, and they are beginning to be seen here; opt for plastic.

Mexican tributes

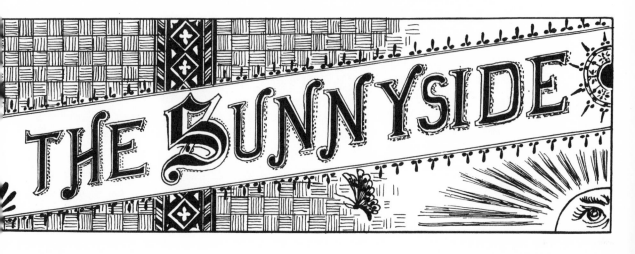

PRINTING AND THE WORD

The visible word of English death is in a sad state today, very thin. In the seventeenth and eighteenth centuries, an invitation to a funeral could be a simple statement of time and place, or ornamented with skulls, enthroned skeletons, scythes, hour-glasses, pennants, hatchments, and sometimes a whole funeral procession. These elaborate invitations were generally stock engravings on wood or copper with a blank space for the printer to add details. They went out of fashion in the 1840s and memorial cards took their place, sent out after the funeral with the number of the grave in its cemetery, instead of the name of the church for the service. Again, there were stock blanks, embossed and pierced, at once elegant and tough, with the blank space for the printer to fill. Most of this later printing was weakly done on the splendid cards, but there were a lot of fine sentiments to be crowded in (perhaps making an acrostic on the name of the dead), and the general effect was still rich. Here, the gothic style was as firmly entrenched as baroque was for the hearse, but understandably because gothic was the current religious style, and the thick black letters gave weight to death.

On these cards the emblems of grief were beautifully designed; the skulls and skeletons were replaced by sarcophagi, both Classical and

Left. The Pearly Gates again; metal frame to hold memorial card. Probably continental, late nineteenth century. *Above.* Title of an undertakers' journal. United States, late nineteenth century (see page 141)

135

Egyptian, urns, willows, mourning angels and cherubs, broken columns, inverted torches, ivy, gothic architecture. The dies must have been made of steel, and foliage and architecture are very crisp, but there is a chubby quality in the figures that recalls wooden gingerbread moulds. Some cards are white with black borders and perhaps the backgrounds pierced out. Some have black backgrounds and white or grey borders. Makers' names are Mansell, Wood, Haddon. Some of them were clearly designed in the 1840s, though the funeral dates may be in the eighties; others were designed later in the same tradition with additions like black paper-lace edges and gold printing. At the height of the fashion, in the fifties and sixties, fretted mounts were made for the cards, repeating the same motifs, in heavier cardboard to be framed or in metal with gates to open in front of the card and a strut to stand it on the mantelshelf. By the nineties, lithographed cards, folded, with the memorial message inside were in general use, printed in black, silver and muted colours with a different range of designs – violets, daisies, bigger ivy with backgrounds of marble, banners, turned corners; everything is much more realistic, though there are some Edwardian cards, black with white motifs and narrow borders, that might easily have been designed in the 1930s.

In the nineteenth century, the cross appeared very little, today it is on a lot of the cards, slanted, decorated with flowers, wreathed with bay. New flowers like cyclamen crop up and there are drawings of sunsets, windows with rays streaming through, and gardens of remembrance.

Flower-cards are a new invention. The sender of a wreath used to write on his own visiting card, and the florist kept a stock of plain or black-edged cards for people who had none. Today these are rare – most florists have cards with printed or engraved copperplate messages – You Are Not Alone, Deepest Sympathy, From Friends and Neighbours, Suffer Little Children to Come Unto Me – and flowers or crosses in the corners, sometimes with colour-printing and embossing. At the bottom can be the name of the florist as large as the sympathy, and even the Interflora symbol. Newest of all are small cards brightly and badly printed with flowers in colour. These come in boxes from America assorted with birthday, wedding, get-well, die-soon messages and they save trouble, the florists say.

The Order of Service used to be nicely printed in a little book with round corners, padded leather covers, In Memoriam in gold, and gilt edges. Each cream page was enclosed in a scarlet rule with fleurs-de-lis

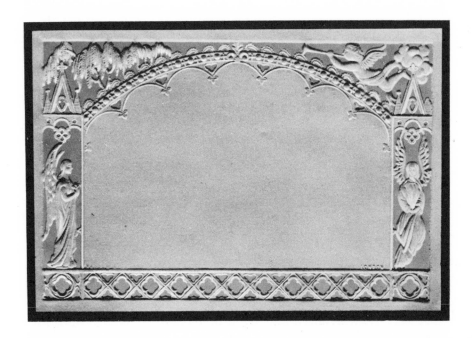

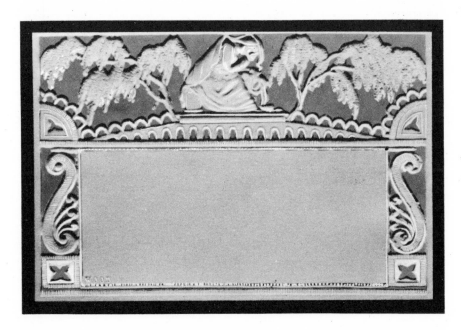

Printers' blanks for funeral cards, embossed and cut. England, mid-nineteenth century

YOU ARE
NOT
ALONE

FROM

B. COLES, FRUITERER & FLORIST, MARKET ST., SALISBURY
TELEPHONE 2260

Suffer little children to come unto me

From

B. COLES, FRUITERER & FLORIST, MARKET ST., SALISBURY
TELEPHONE 2260

Cards to accompany flowers to the grave. The printer supplies these to the florist. Sometimes he carries a large stock. They are often en-

In Memoriam

B. COLES, FRUITERER & FLORIST, MARKET ST., SALISBURY
TELEPHONE 2260

In affectionate
Remembrance

from ....

graved and the bottom two
on the right-hand page were
originally printed in colour.
England present day

From

From

B. COLES, FRUITERER & FLORIST, MARKET ST., SALISBURY
TELEPHONE 2260

THE UNITED STATES TYPE FOUNDRY, JAMES CONNER'S SONS, NEW YORK.

163

at the corners, and the book had a gothic title-page, moiré end-papers, and decorated initials. A cheaper version had purple cloth and less gold. Now, more and more of them are bound in stiff paper or are folds of card with the service abbreviated to fit. However truncated, they are on one side of a social line cut somewhere through the middle of the middle classes, above which the Order of Service is used, below which, the memorial card. The undertaker both in England and the United States knows exactly which to offer.

A lot of people feel that a personal 'letter of condolence' (these are not yet printed) demands a personal answer, but printed cards with thanks for sympathy are very common, and there is a new line in England combining memorial card and thanks, a fold of rich embossed card like a wedding invitation, with an initial, and 'In Memory', and dates on the outside, and 'Thanks for Sympathy' inside. This has not yet achieved exact class stratification but is more widely used in the north.

In England 'registers' are larger folds of card given by the undertaker for recording the names and addresses of those who sent flowers, and the nature of the tribute. In the United States they are to list 'Friends who Called' to see the body, and can be very lavish. They lie open on a standing desk for the visitors to sign.

The writing-paper, bills and visiting cards of undertakers in the eighteenth and nineteenth centuries were often magnificent, solemn and heavily ornamented, the heading sometimes filling more than half the sheet. Now, they might be any tradesman's stationery, except for a rare burst of purple, and usually 'Funeral Director' in gothic survival.

All through the nineteenth century both undertakers and mourners, but not sympathisers, used black-edged paper and envelopes, the borders getting wider down the social scale and across the channel, reaching their maximum in Belgium, where the border was often an inch wide and where also black doilies were used for funeral food.

Undertakers' trade papers are, of course, not seen by clients and so do not have to be gothic, but can follow the normal trends of printing fashion, as may be seen in the back numbers of the American undertakers' magazine, *The Sunnyside*.

It traces perfectly not only the fashions in printing, but also the expansion of a bright new trade. In 1885 there are columns of jokes – 'Fitful Flashes' – 'A healthy girl is generally well maid' and 'It's a coal day when wood gets left' – and happy information – 'H. N. & C.'s magic

Catalogue page of printers' stock blocks for undertakers' and masons' cards, writing paper, etc. (Cooper Union Museum). United States, mid-nineteenth century

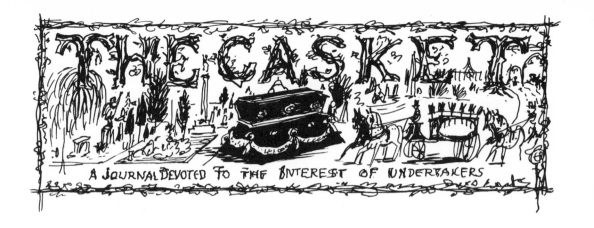

A JOURNAL DEVOTED TO THE INTEREST OF UNDERTAKERS

Its Mission: to Educate, Organize and Give the Lead

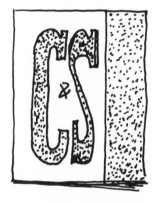

Titles of United States undertakers' journals. *Above, top. The Casket*; founded in 1876, with a lovely ideal necropolis background. *Below.* Another title of *The Sunnyside,* early twentieth century. *Left.* Four covers used after the two papers merged; not drawn to scale. *Right.* An advertisement from *Sunnyside,* 1886

A WORD OF WARNING!

There are many styles of Caskets, each represented to be "Just as good as Stein's!" THEY ARE NOT! but, like all Counterfeits, lack the peculiar and remarkable qualities of the genuine.

The following quotations will be recognized as a few of the modest (?) Claims of our competitors. We append the popular criticism applied to Stale News.

"Just as good as Stein's" — Strike the Gong!!

"The Thumb Screw is Doomed" — Toll the Bell!

"OUR Elegant Copper Metallics" — Sound the Alarm!

"OUR Reliable Telegraph Key" — Push the Button!

"OUR Fastening Attachment" — Did you Ring?

"OUR New Detachable Hinge" — Pull the Cord!

"OUR Zincoid Copper Linings" — Crash the Brass!!!

"OUR Screwless Top Moulding" — Agitate the Metal!

The Originators of Every Practical Idea now used in connection with Burial Caskets. WE CAME! WE SAW! WE CONQUERED! and we still hold our several forts at 13 Bond St, New York; 81 Union St, Boston; Grand Supply House at Rochester, New York.

Stein Manufacturing Company

hair restorer rubbed on a corpse takes *off* hair!!!.' The typography is tough and telling, and there are violent and splendid blocks. Embalming is minutely discussed. Grant's casket was vulgar – 'Pshaw,' exclaimed Mr Dieckman warmly. 'The Standard Fluid made as fine a corpse as we ever buried out of drowned and badly blackened body, the thermometer 102.' – 'For delicate skin, I speak of Clarke's fluid (my own).' There are

THE
ORIENTAL EMBALMING FLUID!

HULLO! HULLO!! HULLO-O-O-O!!!!
AS A PERFECT
Embalmer, Bleacher & Deordriza
THE ORIENTAL
Today stands unequalled.

Another advertisement from *Sunnyside*

chatty bits about gloves, plumes, hearse-horse-nets, candles, preserved natural flowers, Italian wheat, and Cardinal McCloskey's burial in 'rich-hued San Domingo mahogany, with circular ends . . . covered with heavy royal purple silk plush. It was lined with the finest purple satin, tufted and pleated most artistically. The body was not placed in the casket . . . Instead, the remains rested on a cedar, oval-shaped board covered with shirred purple satin, which board rested on the coffin. The Cardinal's head rested on a beautiful purple silk pillow, on which, embroidered in rose-coloured silk floss, were the words Cardinal McCloskey. Gold urn screws and gold extension handles beautified the casket. The effect was augmented by heavy bullion fringe, and tassels and rosettes of the same.'

1886: everything was in transition; today's practices can be caught glancing by – routine embalming of the corpse before cremation, package-deal costing, the 'Kentucky Association's' name changed from Under-takers to Funeral Directors . . . and then abruptly – 'A Ghost three feet high, wearing a velvet suit and hat is frightening North Haven, Cf. A labourer declares he cut it in two with his spade.'

1888: side by side with the crowded advertisements, full of blocks, Egypt, and quotations from Shakespeare, and the copy that delights and puzzles us today – 'A revolution in coffin-making. Grand Triumph of the Canons of Art over the Toy Pop-Guns of Rival Manufacturers' – the smart stuff starts – a half-page entirely blank except for a small message in the middle:

Just too Busy for Utterance
John L. Clarke
Manufacturer, Jobber, and Importer
Providence R.I.

1889: Golden Oak is IN for caskets – and there are two good ads: 'Make a Date each month for looking over your stock of fluids and supplies.' This accompanies a merry widow with the reins of a spanking pony in her tiny black-gloved hands and an empty seat beside her: and there is a truly terrifying photograph of a child, Howard Paxton Keates (age five years) of Jeffries & Keates, Atlantic City: he is saying 'This baby will keep all right for a couple of weeks. Primero is all right,' and he is em-balming a doll.

1900: through the early nineteen hundreds, the linings and quiltings and fine blocks of hearses and handles go on, Colleges of Embalming begin, burial shoes are established. By 1912 the magazine is printed on art-paper with half-tone illustrations and there is an Egyptian heading on the title-page. Beautiful motor and electric hearses are advertised, there is demand for sterling silver casket hardware, and pretty-girl advertisements – 'To preserve such delicate beauty as this. . . .' An undertaker in Cleveland has a modern mummy standing in the shop (all are welcome) to show what can be done.

World War I had almost no effect on the look of the paper; during the twenties there was a new joke column, 'The Funny Side', planes were used to transport and stone-age advertisements replaced Egyptian ones, with cracks about antediluvian methods; and there was an appalling cover (the Funny Side is catching) – a mausoleum in mauve on a granulated ground.

1932: *The Sunnyside* merged with *The Casket*. A new cover was introduced – divided diagonally into cerise and paler cerise with a photograph in the centre. Crushed velvet was IN, and this was the zenith of the draped, quilted and fringed linings. Undertakers' biers looked like early wireless sets, with fretwork sun-bursts.

All pictures of disasters and triumphs had now been purged away, and the paper got steadily duller through World War II; three-colour ads, a Georgian Good Taste cover in the fifties, and a bit of cubism in the sixties. There is still an occasional article on Egypt, good-will-builders are advertised, and dignity is stressed – 'Consider the dignity of your profession and the respect due to the deceased . . . there is nothing dignified or respectful about STOCKING FEET. More and more funeral homes are using burial footwear, regardless of casket style and price.'

For the gentle reader, there is no doubt that *Casket and Sunnyside* shows progressive deterioration in typography, gusto, and ghoul-rating. The aggression of 'Don't Come To Us If You Want FAILURES' has turned into the dignity of shod feet, and the typography has turned with it.

Funeral literature on sale to the public includes the Special Supplementary Number after a state funeral. These are never as lush as English Coronation Specials, which go berserk so that for weeks it is impossible to find an illustrated weekly or monthly without crowns, orb, sceptres, spurs, ampulla, swords and coronations of the past. However, the funeral numbers do very well with purple covers and aerial views of the cortege. They grew with the development of wood engravings to illustrate newspapers, and by the end of the nineteenth century, with the first half-tone reproductions, had acquired a special grey gloom. The *Graphic* for January 26th, 1901, records the death of Queen Victoria. There are three portraits, and a series of black-bordered sombre pages, each captioned the Death of the Queen, with sub-headings – Reading the Announcement at Buckingham Palace, Press Representatives Obtaining the News at Osborne, Outside the Mansion House, and Reception of the News in the West End, all photographically reproduced from wash drawings. Other pages show the Kaiser arriving, King Edward arriving, and the Queen in her Pony Carriage, telegraphing a Jubilee message, holding a drawing-room, last public function, etc. A week later, the next number, twice the price, has a special sad cover (bust of Queen, mourning Britannia, angel with laurel wreath), several pictures of the proclamation of Edward VII, portraits of the new King and Queen and prototype mourning journalism; The Queen as a Woman, The Queen and Music, A Nation's Grief, The Queen and Art, The Religious Side of the Queen's Life, The Royal Mausoleum at Frogmore, The Queen's Homes, England's Three Great Queens, The Queen and Literature, and The Queen's Pets. The Death-of-the-Queen pictures continue, Flashing the News to All Warships, Dawn at Osborne, Sympathetic Callers at the British Embassy in Paris, Receipt of the News in Soho. Again a week later, black bordered, the Funeral Number with double-page spreads of processions, train, lying-in-state, and service. Articles on Last Scenes at Windsor, the Queen's Descendants, The Floral Tributes, The Etiquette of Court Mourning, and Royal Burial Places.

The longest-lasting words for the death of an ordinary man are on his tomb. These range from poems by poets for poets to the single word; as usual, the fewest words are the most powerful – SCHMIDT, FATHER, MOTHER or MY SON. These carry more emotion than the oily sonnet to virtues – not always the same emotion. A compelling example is the tomb put up in Kensal Green by the chef, Alexis Soyer, to his wife. Cherubs support a pretty 'Gainsborough' bas-relief of her, with a palette hanging on ribbons beneath, while her real palette is mounted behind glass on the back of the tomb. It is inscribed TO HER in heavy letters nine inches high. Sometimes the lettering of epitaphs is wonderful, but they could only be reproduced properly in the largest of coffee-table books, so here are some of the words without the style. Usually there will be what are called

WORDS, a few nice WORDS, perhaps a message from the Bible or the poets, or more rarely an individual epitaph.

Words for Tombs

AT REST. REST IN PEACE (or R.I.P., or REQUIESCAT IN PACE). SLEEPING PEACEFULLY. IN MEMORIAM. NIRVANA. WITH AFFECTION. NOT LOST BUT GONE BEFORE. TENDER MEMORIES. COMETH UP AS A FLOWER. IN HOPES OF A RESURRECTION TO ETERNAL LIFE. IN HEAVEN. CALLED HOME IN THE MORNING OF LIFE. THY WILL BE DONE. ALWAYS IN OUR THOUGHTS. PEACE. SAY ONE ROSARY.

Lettering on tombs. *Above*. Portugal, 1960. *Below*. New England, 1881

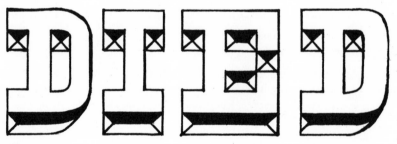

Epitaphs

BEHOWLDE YOURE SELVES BY US SUTCH ONCE WERE WE AS YOU
AND YOU IN TYME SHAL BE EVEN DUSTE AS WE ARE NOW.

St Bartholomew the Great
London, 1558

REMEMBER ME AS YOU DRAW NIGH
AS YOU ARE NOW, SO ONCE WAS I.
AS I AM NOW, SO MUST YOU BE,
PREPARE FOR DEATH AND FOLLOW ME.   Wolfpits, Connecticut, 1830

FULLER'S EARTH.[1]   JAYNE, DEAR CHILDE.

HERE LIES A SPORTSMAN, JOLLY, KIND AND FREE
FROM THE CARES AND TROUBLES OF THIS WORLD WAS HE
WHEN LIVING HIS PRINCIPLE AND GREATEST PRIDE
WAS TO HAVE A FOWLING BAG SWING BY HIS SIDE
AND IN THE FIELDS AND WOODS TO LABOUR, TOIL AND RUN
IN QUEST OF GAME WITH PERO, COBB[2] AND GUN.
BUT NOW POOR MORTAL HE FROM HENCE HAS GONE
IN HOPES TO FIND A JOYFUL RESURRECTION.

                                        Southwell Minster

THE EARTH GOES TO THE EARTH, GLITTERING IN GOLD,
THE EARTH GOES TO THE EARTH, SOONER THAN IT WOULD:
THE EARTH BUILDS ON THE EARTH CASTLES AND TOWERS,
THE EARTH SAYS TO THE EARTH — ALL THIS IS OURS.

                                        Melrose Abbey

IN MEMORY OF
Mary Wife of
JAMES PINK
FOR NEARLY 50 YEARS
THE FAITHFUL SERVANT OF
MRS GRIMES
THIS STONE IS AFFECTIONATELY RAISED

                            Shorwell, Isle of Wight

HERE REST THE SILENT DEAD, AND HERE TOO I
WHEN YONDER DIAL SHALL STRIKE THE HOUR MUST LIE.
LOOK ROUND! IN ORDERLY ARRAY
SEE WHERE THE BURIED HOST AWAIT THE JUDGMENT DAY.
STRANGER, IN PEACE PURSUE THINE ONWARD ROAD,
BUT NE'ER FORGET THY LAST BUT LONG ABODE.

                        St Just-in-Roseland, Cornwall

HERE REST THE HOPES AND ASHES OF JOHN CLARE.

TO THE MEMORY OF THOMAS PORT

Son of John Port of Burton-upon-Trent in the County of Stafford, Hat Manufacturer who near this town had both his legs severed from his body by the RAILWAY TRAIN. With the greatest fortitude he bore a second amputation by the surgeons & died from loss of blood. August 7th 1838. Aged 33 years.

> Bright rose the morn & vigourous rose poor Port,
> Gay on the Train he used his wonted sport.
> E'er noon arrived his mangled form they bore,
> With pain distorted & o'erwhelmed with gore:
> When evening came, to close the fatal day
> A mutilitated corpse the sufferer lay.

The American West

DAN DOWD
RED SAMPLE
TEX HOWARD
BILL DELANEY
DAN KELLY
LEGALLY HANGED
1884

JOHN HEATH
TAKEN FROM
County Jail &
LYNCHED
By Bisbee Mob
in TOMBSTONE
Feb 22nd 1884

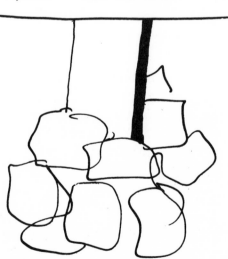

OUR TOOTSIE. OUR LITTLE DARLING. MISS BAMBI BLAIR. MIKE, TRUE BLUE. OUR PET CAT SMITTY. COLONEL. SANDY THE ARISTOCRAT. BABY MOUSETTE. OUR BABY CZAR. SNEEZLES, HE WAS GREATLY BELOVED. LORD DANDY. BUDDY BUMPS. POOCH. ZULU. TINY TIPPY. MY PAL SCHMOOLIE BOY. TIGER DAN. ONE EYE, SHE LIVED TO LOVE. BILL: THEY CALLED HIM A GENTLEMAN. MUMMY'S OWN TOY. ALAS POOR FANNY. GO TO SLEEPIES BOY. 'PIP' AS SHE HAD LIVED – DRINKING TEA BLESS HER. IN MEMORY OF A DEAR LITTLE TORTOISE PET OF THE FAMILY. IN LOVING MEMORY OF SUSAN OUR WEE DARLING WOOLLY MONKEY. HITLER, IN MEMORY OF A GOOD AND FAITHFUL PAL.

JOSSER
May 1935 – May 1950
Age 15 years
'Passing Years will never Dim,
The loving memories we have of him.
We are proud to know our little mate
Is nesting peacefully among the great.'
'RUB YOU' NOSE'
CAT

Mary of EXETER
awarded Dickin Medal
for outstanding war service
1940–1945

How we love you 'Witty Woo'
Husband cat of 'Sunny Boo'
Father of Blue Creams, Red
Blues
You-my boy-our British blue –
We took you out to Kenya too
And we played and had fun too
But we brought you home love too
May God Bless our 'Witty Woo'.
'BEECHCOTE SMOKY'

PICOLO I
PICOLO II
MOUSIE
AND
MOPS
ARE WAITING HERE

In Love To
BESSIE BAM
Her Mummy, Daddy and Mi-Mi's
Dear, Good, Little Wuffin Muffin.

The Pets Epitaphs are mixed British and American; can you tell which is which? Answer at end of Notes.

Words for death are getting softer; funerals are cushioned with euphemisms so well established that one hardly hears them sleeking by. Some of them are used only by undertaker to client and are almost meaningless; the change of vocabulary is automatic; I have heard within ten minutes 'fry' to the staff, 'cremate' to me, and 'commit' to the customer. No list could be complete because there are regional differences and elegant variations, but these are some of the words the mourners hear.

Ordinary words	British Euphemisms	American Euphemisms
Dead	Passed Away	Expired, or withdrawn
Corpse	Body	Remains, or Mr X
Funeral	Funeral	Service
Morgue or Mortuary	One of our rooms	Preparation room
Coffin	Coffin or casket according to shape	Casket, now couch (coffin rare)
Undertaker	19th C, funeral furnisher	19th C mortician
	20th C, funeral director	20th C funeral director
Shop	Parlour	Home
Laying-out	Positioning	Helping repose
Hearse	Mr X	Coach
Procession	Cortège	Coach-party
Digging a grave	Working	Opening a vault
Bury	Inter	Inter, or leave
Graveyard	Cemetery	Memorial Park
Embalming	Hygienic treatment	Preservative treatment, or care
Ashes	Cremated remains	Cremains
Burn	Cremate, or commit	Commit or withdraw
Shroud	Robe, or gown	Robe, or clothing
Death certificate	Death certificate	Vital statistics form
Crematorium grounds	Garden of remembrance	Garden of remembrance (for cemetery as well)
Grave	Grave	Space
Looking like death	Going, or terminal expression (medical)	Looking to God
Mourning	Sorrow	Grief therapy
Post-mortem or autopsy	Post-mortem, or autopsy	Necropsy
Money	Cost	Investment

A funeral announcement put up on shops to show that they are closed because of a death. Portugal, present day

....

....

participa...... a V. Ex.ª que faleceu ....

....

....

e se há-de sepultar .... *pelas* .... *horas*

saindo o préstito fúnebre da ....

para o cemitério d ....

    Espera...... que lhe honrem êste acto com a sua presença.

Agencia Magno : Rua de Santa Marta, 56-A-Tel. 4 3189 —Calçada Marquês de Abrantes, 115-Tel. 66 2772—Rua Frederico Arouca, 62-Tel. 08 0022—Cascais

In many trades, code words are used instead of numbers to save time and money in letters and telegrams, and the words chosen usually follow the English romantic bent; so in undertaking. One London supplier lists some of his coffins as Angling, Artistic, Ailment, Agate, Decoy, Decoct, Defend, Frigate, Eager, Faultless, Fascinate, and, for children's coffins, Parrot, Eagle, Hawk, Martin, Owl, Lark, Kite, and Jay, the last flicker of the word of death.

The feeling of both the euphemistic and trading vocabularies is nineteenth century; the word of death has come up from under Sir Thomas Browne. His magnificent hilly and heavy coverings buried everything for two hundred years, and sometimes the remains of the old sonority could be heard even when the brisk style of nineteenth century commerce was well established, as with a cavity-paste named 'Non-Hardening Hercules'. Today, though, people are writing without the urnes.

TRACT

I will teach you my townspeople
how to perform a funeral
for you have it over a troop
of artists –
unless one should scour the world –
you have the ground sense necessary.

See! the hearse leads.
I begin with a design for a hearse.
For Christ's sake not black –
nor white either – and not polished!
Let it be weathered – like a farm wagon –
with gilt wheels (this could be
applied fresh at small expense)
or no wheels at all:
a rough dray to drag over the ground.

Knock the glass out!
My God – glass, my townspeople!
For what purpose? Is it for the dead
to look out or for us to see
how well he is housed or to see
the flowers or the lack of them –

or what?
To keep the rain and snow from him?
He will have a heavier rain soon:
pebbles and dirt and what not.
Let there be no glass –
and no upholstery, phew!
and no little brass rollers
and small easy wheels on the bottom –
my townspeople what are you thinking of?
A rough plain hearse then
with gilt wheels and no top at all.
On this the coffin lies
by its own weight.

      No wreaths please –
especially no hot-house flowers.
Some common memento is better,
something he prized and is known by:
his old clothes – a few books perhaps –
God knows what! You realize
how we are about these things
my townspeople –
something will be found – anything
even flowers if he had come to that.
So much for the hearse.

For heaven's sake though see to the driver!
Take off the silk hat! In fact
that's no place at all for him –
up there unceremoniously
dragging our friend out to his own dignity!
Bring him down – bring him down!
Low and inconspicuous! I'd not have him ride
on the wagon at all – damn him –
the undertaker's understrapper!
Let him hold the reins
and walk at the side
and inconspicuously too!

Then briefly as to yourselves:
Walk behind – as they do in France,
seventh class, or if you ride
Hell take curtains! Go with some show
of inconvenience; sit openly –
to the weather as to grief.
Or do you think you can shut grief in?
What – from us? We who have perhaps
nothing to lose? Share with us
share with us – it will be money
in your pockets.
          Go now
I think you are ready.

William Carlos Williams[3]

And this cautionary notice is also free from all trace of urnes.

THE PROCESSION

Some tribes bury the bodies of their dead until the bones are clean and then take them home again. After a feast, the bones are left in possession, and the hut is sealed and left to fall to dust. In civilized communities, land is too valuable for such tabus to operate. Early burial grounds (which offer the dead a patch about six feet by three instead of the size of a house) will usually be in the middle of the town, but when the town becomes a city good central sites are claimed by the living, and later burial grounds will be on the cheaper outskirts and therefore at increasing distances, entailing long walks for the mourners with the corpse. These long walks have usually been taken as opportunities for display, first emotional and then material – a chance to show them all, goody-goody, a public procession.

The basic pattern of funeral processions is simple and standard, with three ingredients, the corpse, the mourners and the watchers. The corpse gets the finest form of transport; horses or oxen, gorgeous carriages, trains and motorcars have all been used whenever available or invented. Aeroplanes are still only used to move a corpse long distances, helicopters have been neglected but clearly would make beautiful hearses.

The funeral processions of ancient civilizations can be seen in their

Left. The funeral procession of an Australian Bushman. The mourners are painted with white clay, and the bleached bones are carried in a tree-trunk. *Above.* Corpus Christi Day funeral in Naples, early twentieth century, with hooded bearers-of-honour carrying velvet streamers from the pall

paintings and sculpture. So far as this evidence takes us, they were then much like other religious processions, and certainly in Europe the equipment of hearses and special mourning clothes (as distinct from mourning colours) developed slowly, and the nineteenth century, when horse-transport reached its zenith, also saw the most splendid funeral processions.

The special colours spread from clothes to hearses and horses, white in the East, black in the West (with flashes of purple and vermilion and white for children), and coloured the processions, long winding trains, sometimes at night with torches. In England and France the weight of black was greatest in the seventeenth and nineteenth centuries, when draperies abounded, though neither country achieved the baroque splendours of Italy and Spain. For centuries the procession of an English peasant from house to churchyard might consist of the priest, bearers with the home-made coffin, the family behind, and then friends, all walking, and probably with no special mourning clothes at all. The procession of a rich Tudor landowner, though, might have two yeomen conductors, up to a hundred poor men and women as mourners in front of the corpse, all in provided black, two or four horses to the bier, an enormously long pall behind the coffin with attendants in voluminous black hoods, principal mourners who walked if the distance allowed, riding gentlemen, yeomen and servants, still all in provided black.

The elaborate funerals of the seventeenth century led as we have seen to the establishment of undertaking in large communities, and the hire of all the household hangings. In America the situation was a little different; most of the groups of settlers on the east coast soon established elaborate funerals, and America joined Europe in inventing sumptuary laws to disregard; but civilization was always moving west, and pioneer funerals were simple. Those of the dissenting communities still are; to this day an Amish procession is a string of little horse-drawn carriages escorting a plank coffin. Elsewhere, the procession became like all the other aspects of death, more elaborate after the Civil War.

Farther south, in the West Indies, processions were gayer. A missionary account of 1843 describes them in Jamaica as unnatural and revolting in a high degree with wild gestures, drums, and songs on the road. 'On estates, these ceremonies were generally performed in a manner which was, if possible, still more revolting. They took place at *night*, by the light of torches, amidst drummings, dancing, singing, drunkenness and debauchery.' The coffin was carried on the heads of two bearers, 'preceded by a man carrying a white flag, and followed by the intoxicated multitude'. The coffin was put in the grave and partly covered with earth to prevent the corpse following the attendant mourners away from the cemetery. Fowls and other animals were torn to pieces and the flesh and blood scattered in, while the mourners tore their hair and beat their breasts. 'Then home, and cheerfulness reigned.'[1]

By the middle of the nineteenth century tariffs were published in Paris for all classes of funeral. They are wonderfully complete, with prices for serpents, candles, beadles, and bells.

They start *première classe* where *extraordinaire* could cost 7,484 fr, including *Corbillard à galerie argentée, à l'impériale à cinq plumets, avec garniture ornée de broderies, franges à torsades et galons en argent, attelage à six ou quatre chevaux avec harnais drapés et plumets, 300 fr. Baldaquin suspendu à la voûte de l'Eglise audessus du dais, avec rideaux, draperies bordées en hermine, plumets en autruche. Chevaux blancs, extra 30 fr.*

The lists get shorter and shorter, through *5ième classe, corbillard à galerie bronzée, les panneaux drapés, la garniture et les housses de chevaux frangées et galonnées en argent, attelage à deux chevaux, 38 fr,* and still a lot of extras but all scaled down, to *9ième classe, drap mortuaire galonné en fil, devant servir, tant à la maison mortuaire qu'au cortège et à l'eglise. Deux chandeliers argentés, croix et bénitier. Corbillard à panneaux vernis, sans garniture ni housses de chevaux, 18 fr 75* complete, with only one permitted extra, *chevaux blancs, 10 fr.*[2]

In Venice the funeral procession goes in gondolas (see page 99); the hearse-gondola, perhaps another full of flowers, and then the mourners. They row across the lagoons to the cemetery island of San Michele. There is a nineteenth century account of a great Venetian funeral at night with the family's state gondola covered in black velvet and blazing with candelabra. A long train of black velvet spreads behind on the water, held up by tasselled gold cords from the following gondolas, each with a light.

Italian funerals have always been particularly elaborate, especially in Naples where the pall bearers were completely concealed by long robes and hoods. The palls were heavily embroidered, and the elegant coffins decorated with silver; catafalques were crimson, embroidered with a padded gold hour-glass among the baroque scrolls. A specially tragic funeral, such as that of a beautiful young girl, might have the body

Life-size white paper horses ridden by paper soldiers, drawn in the procession of a rich man and burnt at the funeral. China, early twentieth century

exposed in a long white dress on an open shell-like coffin, cross in hands, hair flowing and crowned with roses on a pink cushion.

The enormously long procession of a really rich Chinaman of high rank was, within processional terms, the greatest possible contrast to the heavy baroqueries, for it was bright with coloured and gilded paper exquisitely made into dragons, houses, horses, palanquins and lanterns – everything that the dead man might need in his future life (including huge sums of money) was made for him in paper, to be burnt.[3] The mourners were dressed in white and carried white standards, walking to the noise of bells and cymbals and the dancing of tumblers. Shinto funerals in Japan replaced the lanterns with model trees, either carried or set up outside the house on a very grand scale, made of greenery and hung with long white and yellow ribbons.

Those who have seen funeral processions in Bali say that they are the gayest in the world. Death is seen as the liberation of the soul towards better worlds and higher reincarnations, and the funeral is entirely dedicated to this liberation. A death is announced by a white paper bird with a white paper lamp below it, swinging on a tall bamboo pole by the gate. The ceremonies are always for a number of deaths together, so the corpses are temporarily buried or embalmed to await an auspicious day and the preparation of the animal coffins and of magnificent towers, sixty feet high and based on a turtle and two snakes (the foundations of the world). Above them rises the platform for the corpse, and then wood and bamboo carry up pagoda tiers of paper and silk, decorated with bright ribbons and tinsel and mirrors. Or there are no pagoda roofs, and the towers look like tall cranes clustered on a wharf. They dip and rise in much the same way, for the bearers are full of laughter and drink, and dodge the heavy towers about to deceive evil spirits. At the burning place the corpse is brought down, put in its coffin, and cremated. The towers, though, are kept till evening so that they burn brighter, and everyone feasts all night. Forty-two days later, slenderer towers, white and gold, without colour, make another procession and are burned to help the soul further on its way and to please the judging gods. All the ashes and fragments of these towers are scattered out to sea, and the dead have been purified by air, fire and water to heaven.

In Sumatra, there are wonderful processions by water. From time to time, special boats are carved by magicians, and sent off down river to the world of shadows, crewed by wooden figures representing all the

Left. Large stone containers (some are in the form of ships) for storing the skulls of chiefs. Samosir, Sumatra. *Above.* Si Galegale. Samosir, Sumatra, probably late nineteenth century

people who have died since the last boat-loads. Above the images tower tall bamboo masts with shapes and symbols on them, sometimes rectangles, diamonds, triangles, cones one above the other, very elegant and light, sometimes a carved square or a bird alone. At the island of Samosir, in Lake Toba, are great stone ships, magnificently carved, containing hundreds of the skulls of chiefs, and here too a wooden doll, called *Si Galegale,* dances at the funeral feasts. Dr F. M. Schnitger led an expedition to the island in 1938 and has described the doll, almost life-size, carved from wood with jointed limbs moved by a series of strings. Photographs show its strong sad head with inlaid eyes and movable lids. In the head is a wet sponge, and the doll can be made to weep. It is mounted on a wheeled car. For a child or a chief the doll is made without a head and the skull is used instead, stained yellow with egg-yolk and given eyes of metal or scarlet fruits. The doll is richly dressed and has a horsehair wig and a fine head-scarf. (In the past, dolls were made whose eyes and tongues moved in heads covered with human skin, and also several dolls danced around the stone ships.) The soul of the dead is in the doll and someone sings about his life and virtue. The feasts are always at night, and the mourners begin to dance and *Si Galegale* dances too, embracing them. 'No one who has seen it dancing and weeping in the green mists of Samosir, in a night filled with stars and silence, will ever forget it.'[4]

Everywhere in the world eccentric or special people demand or are accorded special funerals. The accounts of them are exaggerated, to one's sorrow; it is obvious when one thinks about it that remarkable processions will be rare – eccentricity can only find its outlet in such things as can be pre-arranged by the dead; artefacts can all be bought or bespoken at any time and held ready with reasonable hope of success, but mourners cannot be pushed too far, so there are plenty of odd tombs, tributes and hearses, but few peculiar processions; until World War II, though, the burial of a Pearly King or Queen in London really was a most splendid occasion. The Pearlies were costers (or costermongers), street traders with pony-barrows, who during the last quarter of the nineteenth century invented a beautiful and unique costume; ordinary dark clothes were sewn with thousands of tiny mother-o'-pearl buttons, combining geometrical and baroque patterns with crowns, hearts, birds and flowers. The buttons went on to caps, walking-sticks and boots, and the women wore huge swashbuckling hats covered with long bright ostrich feathers. The weight of the clothes is formidable but they were worn for weddings,

christenings, Derby Day, Bank Holidays, and funerals, when the costers
came by barrow from all over London to follow the hearse.

If we assume that there was enough money and no eccentricity, an
urban funeral procession in England during the second half of the
nineteenth century (ignoring local practices such as the coffin carried
on the shoulders in the south and by the handles in the north), would
have gone from the house to the cemetery somewhat on these lines. First
walked two mutes with wands – undertaker's men in black with wide
crape sashes over the inside shoulders and crape draped round their top
hats and hanging down at the back. They carried wands as tall as themselves hung with crape tastefully held in with rosettes at hand level.
Then the feather-pages,[5] one, two, or three undertaker's men carrying
over their heads frames or trays covered with four-foot tiers of ostrich
plumes – there could never be too many classy plumes. Then one or two
boss undertakers, then the hearse. If there were no honorary pall bearers,
mutes, perhaps a dozen or more of them (six being coffin-bearers), walked
beside the hearse wearing black-draped hats and with batons in their
hands. They got drunk at low-class funerals and who can blame them.
The men of the family and close friends walked behind the hearse, and
then came the mourners' carriages drawn by one or two black horses, as
many as were needed, four mourners to a carriage.

The funerals of the great. The same as the funerals of the ordinary –
mourners, corpse, and watchers, but longer, slower, and more archaic.
Some of them have been very exactly recorded; the funeral procession of
Queen Elizabeth I in 1603 was painted, almost mourner by mourner, in
remarkable detail,[6] and is far clearer to us, jet black with white ruffs and
sad pink faces, than the funerals of today recorded in the picture papers.
Other processions were painted, probably for mourners, in several clear
styles, pen and wash or coloured gouache, and weddings and coronations
were done as well, long lines of little figures, sharp on the paper, four or
five inches high, always moving from right to left, so that procession
delineation must have been a profession, and to be left-handed a dis-
couragement.

Queen Elizabeth's procession was headed by Knights Marshalls to
make way, then fifteen poor men and two hundred and sixty-six poor
women, gentlemen, squires, four trumpeters, Rose Pursuyvant with two
Sergeants of Arms and the Standard of the Dragon. The Horse, led by
two Querries, was draped from head to foot in heavy black with gold-

Working-class funeral procession with mutes, feather-tray, and six horses for the hearse.
England, late nineteenth century

fringed panels to the saddle-pad, embroidered coats of arms on shoulder and rump, and plumes of ostrich and heron feathers on the head and tail, plus pennants of lion and fleur-de-lis on the head. (The fine spare heron feathers were once always used as contrast to the rich fat ostrich ones; later the ostrich curled alone.) Behind the Horse walked rows of Grooms of this and that, the Standard of the Greyhound, the Yeomen of every

menial task; the woodyard, the skullery, the poultry, the scalding-house. The Standard of the Lyon. The Horse trapped with velvett. Gentlemen and clerks of the chapel, the banners of Chester, Cornwall, Wales, Ireland, Heralds (a different artist at work here, heads too big). Barons, bishops, earles eldest sonnes, viscounts, dukes, second sons (again a different artist, all too tall), the French Ambassador, the Great Embroidered Banner of England, and heralds with the healme, crest target, sword and coate. The Earl of Worcester, Master of the Horse, leading the Palfrey of Estate with three pennants among the plumes, and Lady Northampton, principal mourner, in front of THE CHARIOTT, drawn by four horses caparisoned in black with pennants at head and tail and coats-of-arms embroidered down the face-piece. Gentlemen pensioners as escort with reversed halberds, twelve banners of arms. The effigy is minutely painted on top of the black coffin, crown, red wig, ruff, chain, orb, sceptre, brocade dress, ermine cloak. The bier is simple, draped in black with a black baldachino carried over it on blue posts scattered with fleurs-de-lys. The Ladies follow, in black with white ruffs, cuffs and stomachers, with wide hooded cloaks to the ground. The Maids of Honour with short veils, Sir Walter Raleigh, Captain of the Guard, and the guard with reversed halberds. The work ends with a lovely painting of the hearse in the Abbey, pennants lining the ogival roof, mottoes and a black cloth fence all round.

The processions marched on in much this way for another two hundred years, and then the great state funerals of Nelson, Napoleon, and later Wellington broke out more black than ever; the nineteenth century was to be tops for death all over Europe, and it was Nelson's funeral in London in 1806 that set the trend; the beautiful hearse was DESIGNED. It was quite small, so that the coffin dominated it, carved front and back to imitate the prow and stern of the *Victory*. The canopy was based on the lid of a Roman sarcophagus with acroteria and black plumes at the corners, carried high on palm-tree columns with light swags, and twists of laurel and cypress.

The funeral was exhausting to a degree unthinkable today, but the pattern was the same. The body lay in state under a black and gold canopy in the Painted Hall at Greenwich for mourners to visit, and it was brought up the Thames on January 8th, at night, in a cortège of nine state barges, the third one with the coffin draped and plumed in black, rowed by sixteen seamen from the *Victory*, three hours to Whitehall stairs, where the coffin was carried into the Admiralty by six admirals, to the sound of guns and the Dead March in *Saul* – that sable music that breaks the national heart, like the Last Post sounded in the Tower of London at night. A long procession took the hearse, drawn by six horses, to St Paul's, where the service lasted for four hours.

Napoleon. Paris 1840. '*Le char funèbre, composé d'un soubassement à panneaux, encadrés dans des colonettes, et orné d'une grande drapérie au chiffre de Napoléon, était à quatres roues pleines et dorées. Sur le soubasse-*

ment, quatorze figures de femmes, représentant nos principales victoires, portaient un cénotaphe orné de la couronne, du sceptre, du manteau impérial; un grand voile transparent de crêpe noir couvrait le tout. Seize chevaux noirs, empanachés, caparaçonnés de housses dorées aux armes de l'Empereur, et attelés par quatre de front, tiraient ce char colossal, haut de onze mètres, long de dix et large de cinq.'[7]

Wellington, London 1852. Probably the most splendid funeral ever staged in Europe, centered on an enormous car made from cannon captured by the Duke, melted by a hundred men in six foundries. It was seventeen feet high, twenty-two feet long and weighed eighteen tons. Even twelve horses failed to stop it sticking in the mud in the Mall but it reached St Paul's at last and is still there, in the crypt. In the procession was every military splendour, the Duke's horse with reversed boots in the stirrups, and one captain, one subaltern, one sergeant, one corporal and five privates from every regiment in the Army. Long panoramas showing it all were engraved, hand-coloured, and sold for souvenirs; the marching men, from right to left, zig-zag interminably, and the great car has an extra flap of paper to get it all in.

Lincoln, Washington to Springfield, 1865. The funeral train was drawn 1,700 miles in fourteen days past 7,000,000 watchers by thirteen splendid locomotives with cowcatchers, huge wood-burning stacks, portraits wreathed in evergreen, and black draperies. There was a bonfire at every station and many farms, and every city had draperies, evergreens, and arches; at each of them the coffin was taken from the train, and through the streets, and opened so that the watchers could see the President's face. In New York, sixteen black horses drew a car draped in black satin, trimmed with silver and lined with white, the canopy topped by a Temple of Liberty and four huge pine-tree plumes made of ostrich feathers. Chicago had a beautiful triple arch inscribed WE HONOUR HIM DEAD WHO HONOURED US WHILE LIVING, REST IN PEACE NOBLE SOUL, PATRIOT HEART, FAITHFUL TO RIGHT, A MARTYR TO JUSTICE, and the city fathers stood to wait in stiff broad sashes of black and silver.

Victor Hugo, Paris 1885. The Arc de Triomphe was draped in crape, with huge swags falling half-way down the arch.

Victoria, 1901. A military funeral planned in advance by the Queen. She died at Osborne on the Isle of Wight, and the coffin was carried on the *Alberta*, through the assembled fleets of Europe with an escort of eight torpedo-destroyers. From Portsmouth to London by train, across

London on a gun-carriage with cream horses and a white satin pall, and from Paddington to Windsor on another train, drawn by the engine *Royal Sovereign*, bearing a wreath of white immortelles bound in mauve ribbon and covered in tulle.[8] Windsor buildings were draped in purple. It was said that no one could be seen on the streets without a bit of black. No one had thought she would ever die.

World War I marked the end of the great black funerals of the nineteenth century and a short-lived fashion for war memorials. Columns and towers and statues had of course often been built to commemorate heroes and battles, but after 1918 a heroic stone was *de rigeur* for every village, and the procession was replaced by memorial services for men buried abroad. Reburial at home was rare.

At the beginning of the second World War burial was gentlemanly; in October 1939 German airmen were buried in England with military honours, lying in state under Nazi flags.[9] Later, they were buried in the extreme corners of country churchyards with no honours. At the end of the war the American authorities reburied all those who had died in concentration camps and been buried in Japanese graves. American reburial customs began in the Civil War, as we have seen; after World War II 225,000 dead were taken back to America.

Since the war, even state funerals have been dull in the west; emotionally moving, perhaps, but dull to look at. The throat-plume of a horse may be changed from scarlet to black, crape put round side-drums, crape

bows on kettle-drums, arms reversed to show that they are carried in sorrow rather than in anger. General Smuts' horse (empty saddle, boots reversed as usual) was led behind his hearse draped in a black net with long tassels. Stalin's coffin was covered in ruched and frilled silk, curious heavy slab-on-slab biers have been used for heroes for the Soviet Union and the bier of at least one president of a collective farm was lashed to a tractor with black bands and bows. But, on the whole, dull.

In 1950, though, the young King Ananda of Thailand was cremated with great splendour in Bangkok. The procession began in the morning. The body of the King was carried in a jewelled urn of pure gold on a gilded chariot about forty feet high and weighing more than forty tons.

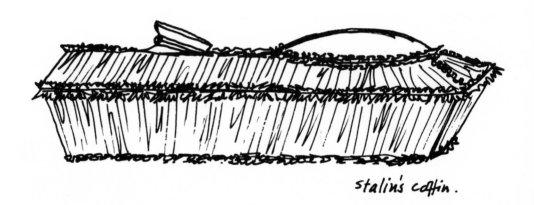

stalin's coffin.

It was made in the middle of the eighteenth century, a tall temple-roofed baldachino on four columns, mounted on five great carved steps, which can be enclosed in scarlet and gold curtains. At the corners were umbrellas, five diminishing tiers like wedding cakes, and attendants shaded the corpse with big leaf-shaped fans. The procession walked to the *meru*, a cremation tower very like the chariot, but larger, equally golden, but ephemeral, and here the urn was lowered and carried three times round the *meru* followed by all the mourners under silk and gold umbrellas, five or seven tiered to show rank, but single for the new King. On the steps of the *meru* were seven-step filigree umbrellas offering the pleasure of elegance instead of shade. After the third circuit, counter-clockwise for mourning, the urn was taken on a lift up to the platform of the *meru* shaded (nine tiers) by an attendant in a tall conical hat. At the top, the corpse was moved from the gold urn to an equally beautiful sandalwood one, and a token fire was lit. Late in the evening, the mourners and dignitaries took tapers to the tower. It was illuminated, and lamps were lit in the golden umbrellas, and the new King lit the fire under the urn. The flames were fed all night till the ashes and bones were pure white under the golden tower.

Eastern processions are calculated for movement, towers are zigzagged or the heavy fans and umbrellas sway, and there are curtains and fringes for the wind. In the west, the aim is stillness. There is heavy music and it is impressive, but not beautiful any more.

THE CEMETERY AND
THE CREMATORIUM

Necropolis is metropolis, smaller. There is the old centre with a temple, trees, and avenues, clot and space together, hundreds of houses built individual and expensive, and the mellow air of fixed habitation. Metropolis has a newer, meaner, conglomeration round the railway station; necropolis a newer conglomeration round the crematorium or a new gate. Both of them have mean reduced suburbs on the outskirts, thousands of little houses only distinguished by the name on the gate and at some seasons by the flowers in front. The only difference is that the metropolitan suburbs are pink with occasional green pantiles and the necropolitan ones are white with occasional green chips.

Necropolis has a long history; where burial was the established way of disposing of the dead, graveyards are found with the earliest cities, and there are specially large ones in Egypt.

Christians, Jews, and Muslims became the tomb-builders and have covered large areas of ground with memorials. Many graveyards are very beautiful and sometimes they are superbly sited. Some of the best are the country churchyards of the British Isles and the eastern states of North America. The reason is very simple; there was plenty of space left for them round the church, which was usually well sited, while in other

Left. Cremation urns. The three in the middle are present day American; the others are English – *top left* and the two floral ones, early twentieth century, the rest present day.
Above. Cemetery gates. England, mid-nineteenth century

countries the secular buildings ran right up to the church except for an open paved square in front, and though the graveyard might be nearby, it was separate and did not have the church as part of the composition.

Moreover, the English (read British if you like, it is what I mean but it always sounds like a trade fair) were not so swept up by the Renaissance that they pulled down all their mediaeval churches, and so we are often centuries in hand with lovely decay. True, a lot of decayed churches were tidied up during the gothic revival, but when the rotting beauty of the churches was at its romantic best, in the eighteenth century, the surrounding tombs that are now at peak were new and raw, so probably now is as good a time as any to see English churchyards: autumn is the best season, when the chestnut leaves are yellow. It is useless to suggest good churchyards, they are everywhere; on hillsides in Wales with slate tombs and very green grass, or round huge marsh churches in Norfolk under twice the normal quantity of sky, or soot-black and white striped near the industrial cities, or full of granite tombs in Scotland. The only place where they are rare is in London, but here we have the great cemeteries instead, compensation enough.

The chancel floors of the churches filled up with tombs during the Middle Ages, and the yards were in use by the seventeenth century. Some of them were soon overcrowded, and sometimes, especially in towns, even the eighteenth-century stones have been uprooted and turned into a fence to make room. The multiplication of the urban population had caused an acute problem in many parts of the country by the end of the nineteenth century; the old burial grounds were full, and books like G. A. Walker's *Gatherings from Graveyards*, 1839, protested about 'the pestiferous exhalations of the dead' from saturated burial grounds. Walker claimed that one inhalation was fatal, that a dog injected with liquid from the ground died, and a gravedigger and fishmonger were stifled by the awful fumes in 1838. He described with envy the catacombs of Paris, Roman quarries under the city, into which removal of the bones from the old graveyards had been started in 1784. They were converted by an architect named Guillaumot to take six million dead, with *Arrête, c'est ici l'empire de la Mort* over the door, boneworks, copies of ancient tombs, and a small pool called Lethe. In 1813 some goldfish were put in, but they died. The catacombs can still be seen on Saturday afternoons, and the visitor is advised '*de se vêtir chaudement et d'apporter quelques provisions de bouche en cas ou l'on serait pris de défaillance dans ces régions froides et humides ou que l'on vint a s'égarer'*. A few pages from an old visitors book survive, and one of them says:

Ici, j'ai reconnu la soeur de mon grand-père
Mon oncle, mon cousin, ma nourrice, mon frère,
Mais, grands dieux, qu'ils étaient changés!
Ils étaient tous en os rangés!

The Tracts of the Cambridge Camden Society[1] listed London's horrors during the eighteen-forties – 'the yet distinguishable features of corrupted humanity left to reek under an August sun, or defaced with the gravedigger's mattock; – churchyard earth carted on to the churchwarden's fields: skulls set up for a mark at which boys may throw their stones; things which the worst and darkest Paganism would have abhorred and revolted from' – 'Nearly the whole of the labouring population in my district have only one room; the corpse is therefore necessarily kept in that room.' Sometimes it was in bed, sometimes on chairs or the floor for several days, and even when coffined still stayed there till the undertakers were ready, being occasionally tapped. A wait of eight or ten days was quite usual, so that the sleeves of the bearers were dripping with the liquid that leaked from the coffin.

Meanwhile, magnificent necropoli were opened during the eighteen-thirties at Brompton, West Norwood, Kensal Green, Highgate, and Abney Park, with plenty of room and regulations. These were cemeteries, not churchyards. They each had one or two chapels, adaptable to any form of Christianity that uses one, but the old huddle of graves round the church was replaced by sweeping landscaped avenues, and a real chance for the middle classes to establish in the best parts either family mausoleums with shelves inside for coffins, or vaults, or at least some splendidly idiosyncratic tombs. Abney Park is the least interesting, except for its Egyptian gates. Norwood is high and airy, Brompton sooty and small. Kensal Green took the West End trade and has a lot of famous people and curious tombs, leading up to a great Doric temple with wings and colonnades for Church of England (the Nonconformist chapel is Ionic). Two of George III's children were buried here to help the social status of necropoli.

Kensal Green is beautiful, and offers the contrast of a long background of gas-works, but Highgate is the best, set almost on top of the hills overlooking London from the north, pitching down below Highgate church.

At the top the Catacombs are cut into the hillside, but open to the sky with Egyptian gates and Egyptian tombs running round; eccentricity was discouraged here, and all is planned. Outside the Catacombs, though, anything went; there is a lion for Wombwell the menagerie proprietor, a piano, a horse, a truly colossal head of Karl Marx, considerable gothic richness, and any number of angels. There are live peacocks, a lot of fine trees, and high grass – the standard of decay is excellent.

All these cemeteries rightly have their constant visitors and sometimes their place in books on London, but the City of London Cemetery and Crematorium at Manor Park (1856) should equally be visited. The contrast with Kensal Green at the other end of London is remarkable. The site is flat, but planted with magnificent planes and one of its chapels is in a most elegant style of gothic, exceptionally good for cemetery architecture. Here the solid merchant worth of the City is symbolized by sheer weight of simple polished granite; there is no fantasy and the most remarkable tomb only has a life-size white marble Descent from the Cross, but there is a curious circus of huge granite books with cord markers, and another of passionate angels (the largest angel is elsewhere, on the tomb of the Elfes, monumental masons). There are also special plots consecrated to the re-interment of the dead taken from some of the scandalous old City graveyards. A good solemn cemetery.

The most ambitious project, though, was the London Necropolis Company's enormous cemetery at Brookwood near Woking, about thirty miles outside the city. It was opened in 1852, and had a private railway station in London adjoining Waterloo, with its own trains, two more stations in the cemetery, and the telegraphic address Tenebratio London. A brochure of about 1901 describes it all, the handsome archway, noble staircase, offices, board-room, drawing-office, and departments for the necropolis, monumental masonry, stables, and complete funeral furnishing. Back at the archway, a carriage road led straight to the 'glass-roofed Station approach, with its white-tiled walls and rows of palms and bay-trees – anything but a morbid effect'. Here were the private mortuaries, and then a marvellous art-nouveau staircase led up to the platforms. The brochure goes on to describe the cemetery with its churches and chapels, and special areas, for different London parishes, Parsees, Mohammedans, Swedes, actors, soldiers, Chelsea pensioners, Oddfellows, Corps of Commissionaires, Foresters and railway employees. Woking crematorium was nearby with full facilities, and the Company had first call on some

The Egyptian-style columbarium at Highgate Cemetery, London. There are serpents and dipped torches cast on the iron doors of the vaults

of the most famous quarries at Carrara. The Company had enough land to sell plots for really high-class building, no shops, pubs or concert halls, no villas, only residences and cottages of taste. There was golf, and the big houses had tennis courts and billiard rooms.

During World War II a landmine fell on the London offices, and destroyed them, with the station, trains, and art-nouveau staircase – everything but the handsome archway. Funerals now go by road, but the visitor can go by train to Brookwood and still see the huge station nameboard, NECROPOLIS, and visit the different parts of the cemetery just as they were in 1901, plus new military cemeteries and new glades of remembrance, and after more than a century, some of the best Wellingtonias in the country.

Most of the big cities of Europe ran into the same trouble at about the same time, and solved it in much the same way, with national differences in planning and architecture; French cemeteries are more formal, laid out on a grid pattern instead of the English winding walks, though, because English landscape gardening became fashionable in France, Père-Lachaise in Paris is half-and-half.

This is a very famous cemetery, much more visited than Highgate, and the disrepair is interestingly different, more of the tombs are made of metal and glass, and ringed with iron fencing, the names of the avenues are on iron standards and there are immortelles everywhere.

One of the finest cemeteries in Europe is Genoa's Staglieno; the architect was Carlo Baralino who died in 1835 before work could start, but his plans were used and the main lay-out and most of the building were done between 1844 and 1851. Mark Twain visited it in 1867:[2] 'Our last sight was the cemetery (a burial place intended to accommodate 60,000 bodies), and we shall continue to remember it after we shall have forgotten the palaces. It is a vast marble colonnaded corridor extending around a great unoccupied square of ground; its broad floor is marble, and on every slab is an inscription – for every slab covers a corpse. On either side, as one walks down the middle of the passage, are monuments, tombs, and sculptured figures that are exquisitely wrought and full of grace and beauty. They are new and snowy; every outline is perfect, every feature, guiltless of mutilation, flaw or blemish; and therefore to us these far-reaching ranks of bewitching forms are a hundredfold more lovely than the damaged and dingy statuary they have saved from the wreck of ancient art, and set up in the galleries of Paris for the worship

of the world.' They are still there in their startling perfection, but multiplied. In the last hundred years the great unoccupied square has been crossed with more arcades, and filled. The Doric colonnades have filled up too. The outermost dusty ring is a dark gallery, with pilasters nine feet apart. Between these rise the memorials, six tiers to each set, black marble between white marble separators one foot nine inches apart. There is a standard pattern for decoration but it is not universal. Lettering is simple and bad. Almost all the wall tombs have lamps, and more lamps stand on the floor slabs. On a Sunday or feast day a lot of them are lit, and there are fresh flowers among the permanent dusty plastic ones, but at lunchtime, even on Whit Sunday, the whole place is empty, and this is a good time to go. Many tombs have carved or photographic portraits, all apparently of murderers or morons, like passport photographs, but in fact normal people – tradesmen, an Indian doctor, an aviator, old ladies in bed with frills. On and on and on, grey and white floors, ochre pilasters, black, and white walls. More colonnades run inside the first, some closed with slabs like the first, and others deeper, open between the columns, holding the wilder memorials, a polychromatic Egyptian tomb split open for a weeping angel to lie on, some Christs, more appalling portraits. Outside, in the sun, there is a grid of cypresses inside the grid of stone with special areas for children, for those who died for liberty, etc; portraits are in black frames painted with white flowers or decorated with coloured lithographed scraps of angels. All the rest of Mark Twain's open space is now full of standard white or black stones.

From this flat campo rises a steep cliff, with cypress-bordered zig-zag ramps and a very steep marble grand staircase up to a pantheon in the middle. On the terrace here, and rising still higher behind, are the luscious tombs of the rich. The Pantheon is circular, with the altar of the Risen Christ in the centre. Under it in another circular room are the elaborate coffins and caskets of the lately dead, in tiers, with strenuous air-conditioning, gold-lettered fringed ribbons, plastic flowers, red and white candles. The throb of the air-conditioning follows one out at the back past a ferny fountain. On up till one can look right down onto the grid and see that there are small tombs along the tops of the colonnades, and here one is among big tombs and rich vegetation. An athlete runs like crazy, held up by scaffolding now, a huge stone angel sprawls post-coitu-animal-gai across a slab, there are some art-nouveau tombs, a captain decorated for bravery at sea sits naked under a discreet wreath and holding the spokes of a ship's wheel behind his back. Small tombs are tucked in on the edge of each ascending terrace; up here, except for one or two sad figures under tempios, rain keeps everything washed clean in contrast to the colonnades where the white statues are so dusty as to seem lit from below. One of the saddest tombs has a life-size old lady in a grey-marble lace cap with a prayer-book in her gloved hands, and every seam and wrinkle in the gloves. She sits on one side of a big cross and the seat on the other side is empty – was it for her husband whose slab is in front and why isn't he there? Family too mean? Too poor? Tastes changed? One tomb is unforgettable, the bronze statue of a five-year-old boy bowling a hoop. The clutching hands of death rise from a crown of thorns behind him as he runs.

Mazzini's tomb is enclosed in a temple full of flags and long red, white and green ribbons, lettered in gold. Opposite is the triumphant crazy tomb of G. V. Grasso, the architect who built it, grinning at his master-piece, and all around are other Risorgimento tombs.

Grasso

Along the grand terrace between the Pantheon and the wooded heights are family tombs, matching cubes with mosaic, Virgins and Christs, interspersed with elaborate gothicries and Egyptian temples. One door is open as we pass; the coffins are on shelves with a lot of plastic flowers, and between them on a stool a mourning mole sits in shirtsleeves and black spectacles.

Lower still is the Tempi di Crematorio – with a list of benefactors, urns, a columbarium and an invitation to join. It does not look very prosperous. Nearby are kept the tower ladders and steps that can be wheeled about to tend the high slabs, and then one is back in the colonnades. The newest of them are by now full of people and the dusty air is twinkling with red lamps, alive with real and plastic flowers.

I have written a lot about Staglieno, and picked out individual tombs which should all be in the next chapter, but it is a remarkable and wonderful place. Mark Twain was right, it stays in the mind, one wants to go back, the palaces are nowhere. Moreover it has most of the ingredients of a modern Christian necropolis; since Italy is a Roman Catholic country the crematorium is, of course, diminished, but everything else is on a very grand scale indeed.

Italy has another superb burial place, the twelfth century Campo Santo at Pisa, a long cloister of extreme nobility, the ultimately calm use of space. The high gothic windows start well above eye level so that the central grass is only seen six times. The east end is raised two shallow steps and the north-east corner deviates to suggest an enormous slow curve from the west. The whole floor is paved with marble tombs, and all along the walls are sarcophagi, slabs, odd pieces of carving and a statue or two. Above these are some fragments of fresco, but most of the wall is pale thin bricks, plain, or whitewashed, or speckled with plaster, and its key of plaited rushes. At the west end is a big tomb flanked by huge bunches of giant chains. The section through the cloister looks square and above is a fine new stark wooden roof, flat. Otherwise, there is nothing at all but the flat tombs in long vistas of space; this, and Nizam-al-Molk's dome at Isfahan, and Durham Cathedral, are our greatest departures from the cave.

All through the nineteenth century good burial grounds were laid out all over Europe and America, large in the growing cities, small in the towns. The small ones are generally formal in plan, and the one at Aviero in Portugal is a good example, a quadrangle laid out in 1860, and

Mausoleums at Aviero. Portugal, present day

beautifully kept up. All round inside the walls are mausoleums, pressed tight, mostly gothic with pitched roofs and pinnacles, and in the centre of one row is a white and gold chapel with a chandelier and a lot of flowers. Inside each are shelves of elaborate coffins, photographs, black ribbons, meticulously watered flowers and plants, and some have curtains. Over some of the doors are carved coats-of-arms, one is draped with mourning, a black rectangle of cloth cut all over with small nicks. Any spaces left in the death-piazza have been filled in recently with futurist-gothic façades in black marble or vitriolite, ready for occupation by the next rich. Within the ring of mausoleums, a marble mosaic path runs all the way round and two more paths cross in the middle, all bordered with hot little box hedges. The centre is full of tombs, earth or elaborate, some with photographs, some with portraits painted on tiles. Sometimes families can only afford to keep a grave for a limited number of years, and then the bones are dug up and put in a small coffin about two feet long in one of a series of small glass-fronted safes, numbered and locked, that line perhaps a whole wall of the cemetery. Inside, there may be lace and plastic flowers and a portrait or a crucifix.

The graveyards in the United States are very like those in England, except that in the country districts there are more burial grounds at roadsides, with no churches near. Otherwise, flowers, monuments and architectural planning hardly differ more than they do in different districts in either country, because of local geography or materials. In both countries a private burial ground or mausoleum used to be quite usual on a large estate, both for convenience and pride, and they are particularly frequent in the southern states of America, with small stones giving a name and date. Box or cypress bushes were planted behind the stone and have now grown into large trees so that the stones are completely hidden. Slaves were usually buried a little apart, and rough stones, about a foot high, stick up without names through the grass.

Most of the big city cemeteries in America were started in the nineteenth century, and combine central best parts with wide winding avenues and crowded straight lines on the perimeter track. New York is a special case; first of course there were the usual graveyards attached to churches in the city, but when these became overcrowded the new necropoli could of course not be placed to ring Manhattan and they are all together in Brooklyn and Queens, acres and acres of the dead of all denominations. Among them is a particularly good Jewish cemetery, built on hilly ground

and jam-packed tight; it is almost impossible to get between the graves. Most of the monuments are tall, and in places it looks like the packed rocks of the Giant's Causeway. It contrasts strongly with the Jewish cemetery in Lisbon where all the stones are very flat and calm.

One of the largest cemeteries in the world is Forest Lawn Memorial Park in California, which offers not only funerals and monuments but a whole range of concert halls, chapels, a cinema, gardens of remembrance for all tastes and a collection of works of art. The largest is a painting one hundred and ninety-five feet long, a Crucifixion by Jan Styka, housed in an 850-seat air-conditioned hall, where some of the annual two million tourists stare at it and listen to a recorded lecture and heavenly music before tottering out to look at the seven-hundred-odd statues (David, Moses, Piéta), and the memorials of film stars.

As well as cemeteries for different religions, there are cemeteries for soldiers, expatriates, and pets. America has a good military cemetery at Arlington D.C., a richly wooded piece of landscaping on a hillside with a fine collection of monuments. Most of them are tough and taciturn, in keeping with the popular idea of a soldier; there are cannons, a block-house, obelisks, pyramids, piled arms, and a few curious spheres and prisms. I have not been able to trace any accepted symbolism for these, nor to find out whether this stone geometry was made at the request of the dead or not. They look very fine, a nice change from crosses, and perhaps are proof of the interesting minds of generals, but Arlington is in fact not at all typical of military cemeteries, where the graves, all with identical slabs or crosses, are usually laid out in rows with mathematical precision. After two World Wars there are a great many of these all over Europe and there are many in America, as hundreds of thousands of dead were taken home from the battlefields. The lines of equal dead leave one stunned and cold, there are too many of them – the most moving military burial grounds are those of the American Civil War because in spite of the terrifying number of men killed, the graves on any one battlefield seem few and small. The battlefields are beautifully and imaginatively tended and sometimes unbearably moving; at Gettysburg one expects this, but one of the saddest is a Confederate burial ground near Appomatox with eighteen small stones. One of them is for a Union soldier whose body was found later and added to the row.

Most of us bury pussy in the garden or leave her at the vets, but many people feel that this is not enough and want to bury their pets in a proper cemetery with memorials.

Here again private ones used to be fashionable. Oatlands Park in Surrey had a shell grotto where the Duchess of York who lived there after 1790 made a graveyard for her dogs and monkeys. Sixty-three pets were buried round the lake by the grotto.[3] Many large estates in England and America have the remains of such cemeteries (I have not seen any elsewhere), but the memorials are usually small and plain. In the public pet cemeteries, though, more emotion may be shown than is usual for human memorials, and grave-goods are deposited, toys and plaster animals on the grave, or a rubber bone or a ball strung to the head-stone. There is a nice little one at Ilford in Essex – a sloping field with standard wooden boards about eighteen inches high, painted cream with black lettering. Among them are some stones, an obelisk, a family plot round a birdbath, and some enchanting miniature tombs scaled down to eighteen inches by twelve, with plants, mousetrap slabs, green chips, and crosses. Outside the lych-gate is a Roll of Honour of the famous animals buried there, Punch (Dickin Medal); Boxer (outstanding bravery against terrorists at Jerusalem); Rex (Dickin Medal); Alsatian (CD rescue dog); Tich (Dickin Medal); Desert Rat; Lewis (mascot goat); and Simon (Dickin Medal), cat of HMS *Amethyst*.

'Le Nini'

Left. Arlington Military Cemetery near Washington, D.C.; a block-house and a cannon.
Above. Graves in an animal cemetery on an island in the Seine

Hartsdale Canine Cemetery, NY, is quite different. It is larger, on hilly ground, beautifully landscaped, with constant visitors tending the graves, admiring the company's begonias, or reading the inscriptions. Most of the tombs are small cubes with a face sheared off for the words, though there are some large stones with carved portraits or photographs on plaques. There are dogs, cats, rabbits, chipmunks, horses, a lion, and people buried with their pets – ashes in an urn on the animal's tomb, or a $13,000 mausoleum – but this is an exception. No attempt has been made at grandeur; the 1896 ironwork entrance gates and railings are light and pretty, and the office is like a park-keeper's one-storey house with a verandah. Inside are many little snaps of nice stout pussies and faithful doggies, a spaniel in red boots and a terrier sitting up in bed in a peignoir with a breakfast tray. Nothing could look more cosy.

It is perhaps unfair to call this 'architecture', but it is *pleasant,* and the architecture of cemeteries and crematoria for English humans is in direct contrast with this. The graves and grass may be beautiful, and calm in the sun and under the trees, but the chapels are almost universally

Right. A rubber ball on a dog's grave in the Pets' Cemetery, Ilford, near London. *Above and two following pages.* Memorials in Hartsdale Canine Cemetery, near New York, present day

awful. The general style is a perfunctory and timid gothic. In most places there is only one chapel, so that it cannot appear either very high or very low, but the necessity of changing denominations with a few props need not have produced such boring buildings. They are transit camps and they look like it.

The cities of the dead get flatter as the cities of the living get taller. Since World War I by-laws have been introduced in England gradually reducing the permitted height of tombstones to three feet or so, and as a lot of vicars object to white marble, and as there are not good stones to be bought anyway, and as two-thirds of the population are still buried, the aesthetic outlook for cemeteries is very bleak indeed; to get a tomb worth looking at today you need persistence, luck and money. The latest and flattest development is the Lawn Cemetery. This carries simplicity of maintenance, which is held to excuse the sumptuary laws (small stones don't crack, fall, tilt over, etc) to its logical conclusion. The stones are now abolished absolutely, and only a small bronze tablet flush in the grass is allowed, so that the motor mower can go straight on over it, a great advance on the previous childishly simple and economical method of keeping churchyards trim by pasturing sheep in them, so that the grass was cropped and the sheep fattened in one almost silent operation. The lawn cemetery has artistic pretensions. It may belong to county or municipal authorities, and will be in open country or outer suburbia, but on a main road. The gates are discreet. Outside, a rustic bus-shelter. Inside, a brick bus-shelter of an office, and ladies' and gents' lavs and a large car-park. There will be trees and possibly a landscaped pond with ornamental ducks and half-a-dozen of the most massive, ugly and uncomfortable wooden seats that money can buy. Beyond lie the lawns with piles of tarpaulined earth and rows of bronze plaques flush with the ground. Most of them have matching flush flower holders, and here and there a few odd tulips or daffs are hanging on. Some of the graves are sunken marshes, some are little tumps – it is hard to fill a hole accurately. The old method of putting back *all* the earth into a grave so that the volume of the coffin became a mound above it allowed for such shrinkage as the nature of the earth demanded and was extremely practical. The mound was often left under grass with a stone at the head, but when the earth had settled, it could easily be razed flat to take a more ambitious tomb. 'Is this lawn sort really easier to keep up?' – 'Well, it's supposed to be, they say, and we shall have rhododendrons next year.'

So this is the expense of spirit in a waste of maintenance, and a waste of good agricultural land as well; burning is more hygienic and saves space in our crowded country and is more in keeping with modern thought, yes? In America, where the first crematorium was opened in 1876, cremation is used in less than five per cent of funerals, but in England, where the first crematorium was opened in 1885 at Woking, cremation is now used for more than thirty-five per cent of funerals, and is going up a steady two per cent each year. The architecture of crematoria, though, is like that of the lawn cemeteries, and they take up the same amount of land; certainly more people will be got into the little pigeon-holes, and some have the ashes scattered anyway, but at the moment one can only feel that there is a sad dumb hankering after necropolis, because the grounds are full of special enclaves – a Garden of Remembrance, Shelley's Copse, Keats' Grove, Forest Green – crying out for splendid monuments instead of the notice, 'Please do not walk in the Long Grass where Ashes are scattered'. All that can be done is to put up a plaque, or to dedicate a rose-tree or a garden seat or a heather plant.

Or there is the columbarium. This is part of the crematorium buildings, in good-taste brick, with bronze lettering and not a flicker of distinction anywhere; even the chimneys are wasted. (There is a richer one in the City of London Cemetery, and a boldly-striped one was built by Claude Gaillard at Père-Lachaise in 1880, but these are not typical). So they are functional and quite right too? The undertakers do not think so; one crematorium has such a low entrance that bearers with a flower-covered coffin on their shoulders always have to stoop for it; another entrance is too narrow; access roads are too tightly curved. I have only heard of one with raised platforms for flowers – elsewhere the flowers are all on the ground in draughty arcades and the mourners must bend double to read the cards. Behind the flowers, the walls are covered with small tablets and a few larger ones, in memory of the dead whose ashes are buried or scattered here. The columbarium proper has tiers of niches where ashes may be put in caskets or urns – these have got progressively smaller as the ovens have got more efficient; once they had to take large pieces of unburnt bone. If you do not want to leave the ashes in the columbarium or the long grass, you can take them home for the mantel-shelf. Beyond the buildings will lie the gardens of remembrance where you may dedicate your plants. In the older crematoria, like Golders Green, there is romantic landscaping, the shrubs will be well grown, the

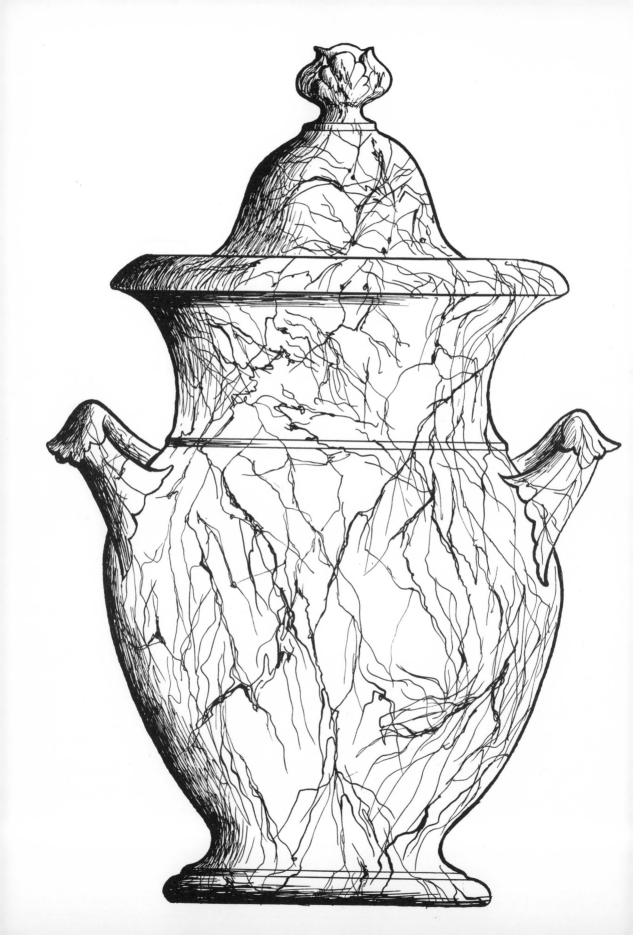

flowering cherry all it should be, and there may even be a few large memorials, but the new places will not allow them and the whole garden may well be crazy paved with flower beds raised in brick for floribunda roses, and those worst of wooden seats.

It may seem as though there is little to choose for looks between a new cemetery, a lawn cemetery, and a crematorium, but the cemetery wins, because although the grave stones are low, you can get a lot of awful variety into three feet; there are the variations of the mousetrap slabs, and there are the epitaphs to read – so they are always worth a look, but they do not add, nor will they ever, the slightest grace to any landscape.

The empty basket, marble.

Left. Earthenware cremation urn, height 17½ inches. England, early twentieth century
Above. Another dog's tomb in Hartsdale

THE TOMB

This is the final word, the lasting praise, the *durable* memento, the paper-weight to pin down the poor soul for ever.

Many peoples have built no monuments at all, making ancestor-figures, or keeping bones, or nothing, but still there are millions of monuments all over the earth, setting out grandeur or faith or conformity, made of granite, wood, gold, cast-iron, plastic, clay, whatever was available or in fashion. We will look at some of them, in chronological order; and also getting smaller.

Back to Ancient Egypt – we cannot escape it – here were the largest and most lasting paperweights of all, designed to preserve the body for ever. We know of about eighty of them – seventy feet square was a small one. The Great Pyramid of Cheops is the one we hear about at school, largest and best, more than 5,000,000 tons of stone on a rock core, 481 feet high, 755 feet square; the base covers over thirteen acres and Herodotus says that 100,000 or 400,000 men took twenty years to build it. Later estimates have reduced both men and time, but still the more we know about the pyramids the more amazing they become, being only a few inches off the perfect square and only slightly off the desired alignment with the cardinal points. All this was calculated with an artificial

Left. Stone tomb near Karachi, Baluchistan. India, fifteenth to seventeenth centuries A.D.
Above. English memorials

horizon – a horizontal bar with a block at one end and a plumb-line hanging from it; a bay – a straight palm-rib with a nick in it – and sledges to move the 200-ton granite slabs.

The palace was nothing, it could easily be rebuilt; the tomb must be eternal, fulfilling the two functions of preserving the body and of storing material goods for the use of the dead man and his *Ka* – his doppelganger, soul, guardian angel, other self, guide, or comforter; we do not quite know what *Ka* was, but cosy to have in any case.

Pyramids developed slowly. The sand-pit burials were liable to disturbance, at least from the wind, and soon the great were nailing down the sand with mud-brick rectangular tombs which held grave-goods as well as corpses. As the buried goods multiplied, the store rooms went underground with the burial chamber.

By the third dynasty, the pyramid shape was established, and Zoser went under a step pyramid 204 feet high. His architect Imhotep has always been regarded as the inventor of building with hewn stone, but the inspiration of the pyramids must have been the increasing bastions of reinforcing brick round the tombs. The inside walls were decorated with incised husbandry ensuring food for the future.

The true pyramid came in the fourth dynasty, and the finest specimens are all of this period, though the pattern went on for another thousand years. Onto their simple geometry and through their galleries and halls has been imposed a long series of most gothic mathematics, telling all future wars and plagues. Doubtless new calculations will soon be made showing that our history on Venus is all predicted in the dark corridors.

The Greeks were much less sure than the Egyptians of a comfortable afterlife, and less concerned with it, so their tombs are simply memorials in basically architectural shapes – slabs, pillars, and small temple-like structures.

The Romans thought that the soul stayed near the tomb and needed survivors and descendants to take offerings of food and wine and flowers. The normal method of disposal was burning, and the Romans evolved the columbarium (still with us), a building which held long banks of niches like pigeon-holes, to take the urns full of ashes. Burial was fashionable but was forbidden within the city, so beautiful architectural tombs spread farther and farther down the verges of the main roads out of Rome, and some of them are still there, narrow pyramids and castles and boxes, large but never overwhelming.

Christian tombs were simple for centuries, because persecution drove the Christians underground for both worship and burial, and memorials were of course small and anonymous. During the Middle Ages the tombs of the great became splendid again, using the decorative extremes of Gothic, and the English cathedrals have some superb ones. A good sort has the carved effigy of a bishop in full panoply supported at eye level on a great bier. Under this lies another effigy of the bishop carved a rotting corpse in his shroud, while above fine crocketed pinnacles soar to the roof of the nave.[1]

Left. Fourth Dynasty pyramid, Egypt. *Above.* Foljambe tomb, Chesterfield, Derbyshire. England, early seventeenth century

205

The spirit of *memento mori* stayed with English tombs, as with the other funeral arts, until the end of the seventeenth century. Then the mood changed and it is clear that the skulls on the eighteenth-century gravestones are decorative rather than minatory; death was handled as gracefully as possible. This was the time for family mausoleums in the park. 'Mausoleum' refers to the tomb of Mausolus at Halicarnassus, one of those seven wonders of the ancient world of which only the Great Pyramid remains. Gradually the word came to refer less to an individual tomb than to a large building holding the remains of an entire family; the Spanish royal family has a magnificent mausoleum made in 1886 at

Above. Carved and painted marble tomb, Lermoos, Austria, mid-eighteenth century.
Right. Carved and painted crest from the tomb of Alice, Countess of Derby, d. 1636, Harefield, Middlesex, probably by Maximilian Colt

206

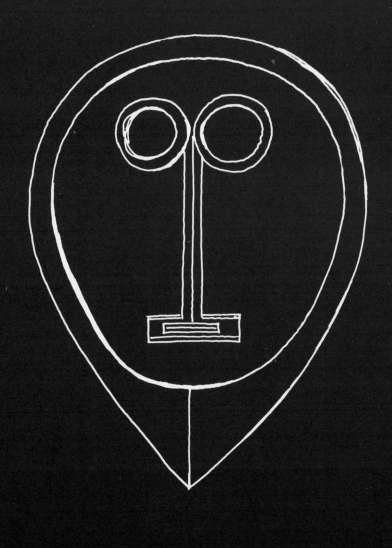

Left. The tomb of Mad Jack Fuller at Brightling, Sussex. It is hoped that he is sitting inside with a bottle and a bird. England, eighteenth century. *Above.* Tomb at Lexington, Mass., 1759[2]

Five types of English eighteenth century tomb. Tombs only moved out into the church-yard when the church was full of them. *Opposite, top left.* Head and foot stones. Some of these are beautifully carved; can be found in most country churchyards. *Top right.* Architectural tombs in many styles are sometimes as much as eight feet high. *Bottom.* A few wooden markers still survive. *Above.* Two rarer kinds. I am told that in the North, anthropomorphic stones were occasionally carved realistically to represent a shrouded figure, but I have never seen one.

211

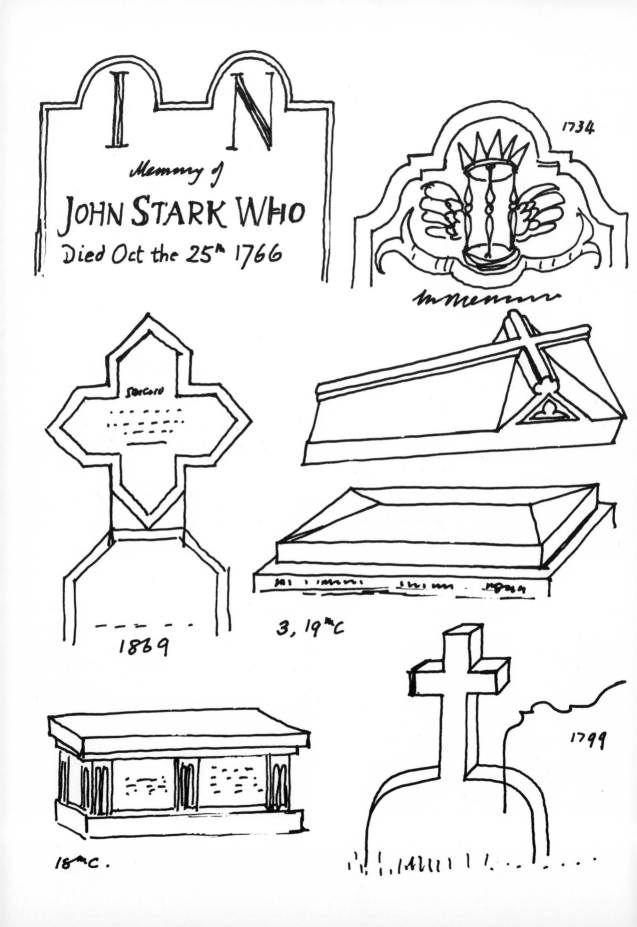

IN

Memory of

JOHN STARK WHO

Died Oct the 25ᵗʰ 1766

1734

Second

1869

3, 19ᵗʰ C

18ᵗʰ C.

1799

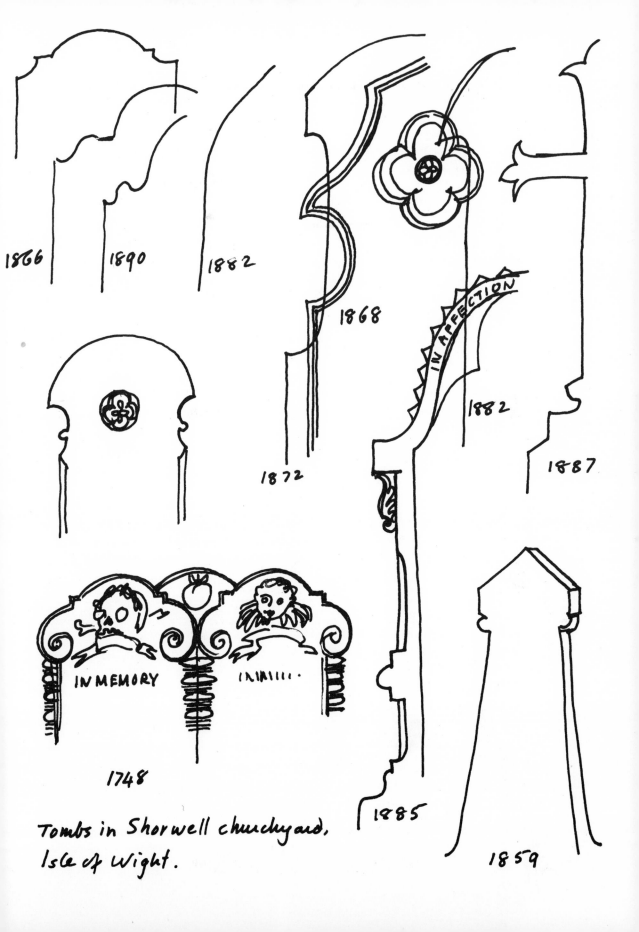

1866   1890   1882

1868

IN AFFECTION

1882

1887

1872

IN MEMORY   ΙΛΙΛΙΙΙΙ·

1748

1885

1859

Tombs in Shorwell churchyard,
Isle of Wight.

the Escorial, matching the pride of the corridor entirely espaliered with family trees, and the black velvet vestments embroidered with silver skulls that were used only for royal funerals. At the Escorial a steep stair leads down to an octagon with the tombs. Everything is made of grey or red polished marble and heavy gold. On each wall are four shelves with the named sarcophagi, thirty filled and two left for the last king and his mother, just right. Only kings, queens and the mothers of kings were put here, and they not immediately, but waiting in rooms off the stairs for twenty or thirty years to become bones. Another mausoleum holds the princes and princesses, a marble corridor with marble openings full of marble tombs receding. One princess has a marble veil carved over her face, and there is a wedding-cake memorial to thirty-two children who died before their first communion. The marble filing system goes on and on, the same but no two alike, each with a hatchment, colours and gold.

Most tombs stand in the air, and the winds bring the world to them, and their sorrow evaporates. Mausoleums are enclosed; they freeze death and isolate it. Grief can be felt even in the famous and splendid ones, like Hawksmoor's for the Earls of Carlisle at Castle Howard. At West Wycombe in Buckinghamshire, a place of diminishing beauty, the Dashwood Mausoleum is a great open octagon, built of flint, standing on the hill behind the church; its atmosphere chills the visitors climbing up from the caves where wicked stories of the Hell-Fire Club are son-et-lumièred in the caves underneath.[3]

Mausoleum-building went on during the nineteenth century; Frogmore at Windsor Castle, the one for Sir Titus and Lady Salt at Saltaire, and another at Warter, also in Yorkshire, are all special. One of the most beautiful, though strictly a mortuary chapel and not a mausoleum, is the one built by Mary Fraser Tytler at Compton in Surrey after the death of her husband the painter G. F. Watts, in memory of all who rest near. She and the villagers baked its bricks and she designed it and they all built it, byzantine and blood-red. Inside, it is glittering art-nouveau, with gesso angels enclosing the walls with their wings. Watts is buried in a colonnade up the slope, and there are some good terra-cotta tombs to his friends.

After decorative death in the eighteenth century, the romantic movement early in the nineteenth made melancholy and mourning chic again, but the symbols were different and the skull never regained its old supremacy; it was replaced by the willow which, at least in Wales, lingered well into this century.

After the romantic movement came the massive and idiosyncratic tombs, the fine flower of nineteenth century assertiveness. They can be seen in thousands of burial grounds all over Europe and America. The one which stays most clearly in my mind is one I never drew, a monument in the Montparnasse Cemetery in Paris to the inventor of a patent lamp. It is a full-size double bed, sheets and all. The inventor and his wife are sitting up in it side by side, she in a frilly nightdress, he in full evening dress, holding up his lamp.

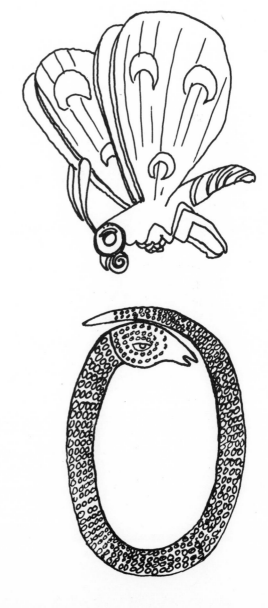

Above. Large cast-iron tomb at Bridgnorth, Shropshire
Right. Symbols. A butterfly from England and a snake from Austria

Opposite. 'No. 5 Massive cast iron Tomb, on heavy octagon base, on which is a circular pedestal with ornamental buttresses, with finely modelled figures, surmounted with obelisk; applied ornamentation throughout, the whole fitted complete.' 9 ft. 5½ in. by 4 ft. 5⅜ in. It was supplied 'painted stone-colour, bronzed, or enamelled in imitation of granite or marble, the figures and scrolls in real bronze metal, stained; also the torches, chaplets and other applied work.' *This page* (*a and e*) Tombplates, painted stone-colour or varnished black. (*b*) Cemetery plate NO DOGS ALLOWED IN THIS CEMETERY. (*c*) Tomb cross, painted or varnished. (*d*) Cemetery number plate. (*f*) Cross No. 5, coping HH, freize 28, with corner terminals. All from the catalogue of the Coalbrookdale Company. England, 1875

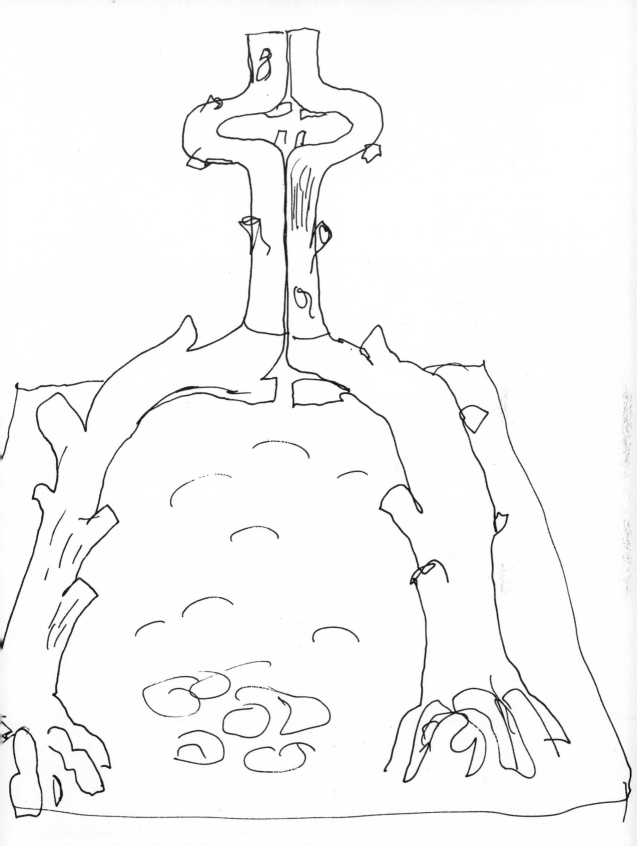

Left. The postman Cheval built his own tomb at Hauterives in France in the style of his Palais Idéal nearby. *Above.* Tomb at Aviero, Portugal, 1884

Decorated for Independence Day. This type of tomb, a large family memorial with individual footstones, is more common in America than anywhere else.

Left. Memorial to a newsboy, with fountains, in Great Barrington, Massachusetts, erected by public subscription. *Right.* The family tree is a pleasant nineteenth-century conceit (see page 182). This one is in Lowenburg, Silesia

221

Left. Inflated Granite (Mausoleum in a Buffalo, New York, cemetery). This is one of two solid granite benches placed near the large and imposing marble and glass mausoleum erected in the 1880's for the only son of one of the oldest, and most prominent, families of Buffalo, New York. (For the story behind this mausoleum see note below.) The benches were 'streamlined' before this word had even been invented – and the granite seems actually inflated

Above. Sketch of the whole mausoleum

Next page. The Vision of Dead Desire (Mausoleum in a Buffalo, N.Y., cemetery). The only son of this family, it seems, had been carrying on a love affair with a beautiful maid in the family's employ. In an effort to break up the affair, the parents packed him off to Europe, where he shortly died. Overwhelmed by remorse, the father and mother had the mausoleum erected, and large marble replicas of *themselves* were placed within it. . . Here we look within the mausoleum (the figures of the father and mother are beyond the scope of the picture) – but we discover the figure of an angel (who is said to represent the maid!) hanging over the replica of the dead son – the whole mise-en-scène having the quality of a disturbing vision . . . *Notes by Clarence Laughlin* 223

The tomb of Sir Richard Burton[4]

Er Serehog Gof Am

ABRAM PIERCE

1926

TREFRIW
N. WALES
SLATE
TOMBS

AM ABRAHAM MAB

1880

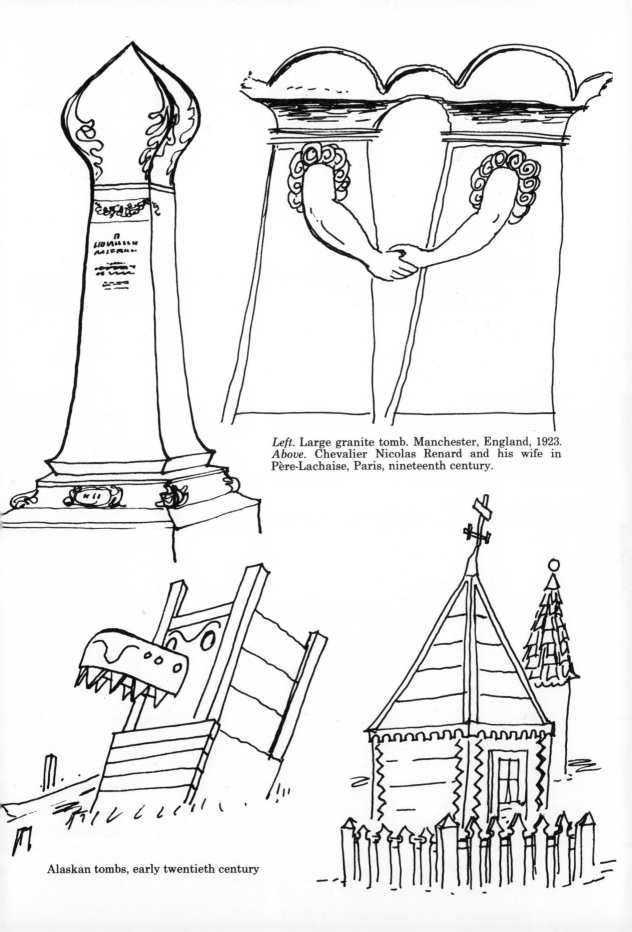

Left. Large granite tomb. Manchester, England, 1923.
Above. Chevalier Nicolas Renard and his wife in
Père-Lachaise, Paris, nineteenth century.

Alaskan tombs, early twentieth century

The Macabre Bird (Louisiana Rural Cemetery). The swamp cemeteries of Louisiana contain a type of folk art which is unlike anything elsewhere in the U.S. This kind of folk art usually takes the form of boxes made of wood and glass — which are placed

Today, we have such small tombs as the by-laws and the parish councils and our diminished interest allow. Occasionally, a special tomb will be carefully made to tell us something about the dead, but few people merit a carved portrait, lion or piano, and most mourners know this, and are content with the standard symbolic carvings of the monumental mason:

ANCHOR	Hope (sometimes used for a sailor, of course)
ARCH or GATE	Entry to heaven, or victory over death
BUTTERFLY	Resurrection
CLOVER LEAF	The Trinity
CROSS	(Celtic) Immortality
CROSS	(Greek or Latin) Christianity
CROSS	(Latin on 3 steps) The Trinity, or Faith, Hope, and Charity
CROSS	(Maltese) Bravery
CROSS	(St Andrew's) Martyrdom
CROWN	Reward in heaven
DOVE	Peace, or the Holy Spirit
HOUR GLASS	The flight of time
IVY	Remembrance, or friendship
LAMB	Purity (sometimes used for a child)
LAMP	Knowledge of God
LAURELS	Fame
LILY	Purity
OROBUROS	(Snake swallowing his own tail) Resurrection
PALM	Victory
PASSION FLOWER	The Passion of Jesus Christ
PHOENIX	I will rise again
SHELL	Pilgrimage
ROSE	Sweetness, or the Virgin Mary
SWORD	Victory, Justice or Mercy
VIOLETS	Humility
WHEAT	Fruitfulness (if used for the old – gathered in)
WILLOW	Grief

Most of these are common in Europe and America, and most of them suggest belief in survival after death, while the broken column, draped urn, upturned torch, skull, and scythe, symbolize only death.

The most usual tombs in England and America today are headstones, mousetraps, and curbs. The headstone comes in many sorts, and may

before the plastered brick tombs, raised above the marshy earth – and intended as memorials for the dead. The contents of each of these boxes is unlike all the others. But in some boxes birds are used (a type of swamp dove, which is stuffed, and used as a symbol of the Holy Ghost) – the birds never being arranged in quite the same way. This one, with its red eyes, and singed wings, is particularly strange and macabre – floating above the conventional religious figures below – and seeming, somehow, to suggest the feeling of the albatross in the 'Rime of the Ancient Mariner' . . .   *Note by Clarence Laughlin*

heavenly gate.

a
mousetrap

"from Neighbours"
black tin, gold gothic

height - 2'6"

chips
marble
earth

SMITH

Ten tombs and two flower-holders. England, present day

231

have a smaller footstone or a curb as well, or both; it is the oldest traditional design, but many of the variations are new this century. The cross was a nineteenth-century fashion now losing ground, and the curb was popular from the end of the century, though the mousetrap, which needs neither plants nor chips, is replacing it in favour now. All of them can be got in marble, granite, or various stones. Wood is used as well, and plastic – black, white, pink, or pale blue, with do-it-yourself gilt letters – is reported from South Africa.

Tomb with lantern. Portugal, present day.

Nineteenth-century graves were often planted – 'The Turks, like the Welsh, adorn the graves of their friends by planting flowers upon them, often the myrtle but sometimes the amaryllis'[4] – but flowers or even shrubs need attention, and the old habit of going to the grave on Sunday has died out. Shortly after World War I, it was seen that the occasional nineteenth-century custom of filling in a curb with trouble-free marble chips could be revived and brightened. The first successfully dyed chips (smaller than the Victorian ones, like the tombs) were green for grass, but they now come in a range, including blue, old rose and a lovely lilac.

Ice-lolly tombstone. Vancouver, twentieth century

RELICS AND MEMENTOES

Preserved corpses are generally private, but sometimes, like Lenin in Moscow, they are publicly preserved as cult images, either visible so that the adoring eye may see the very flesh, or magnificently enclosed.

The bones and hair and clothes of Christian saints have been kept in rich reliquaries for centuries. These may be rings enclosing a small finger-bone, or even a bone-chip, behind a crystal cover; gold cases for limbs; jewelled sarcophagi; or, for very popular saints, whole cathedrals. For an intermediate example, Santa Maria Maddelena in Rome is a good baroque church which preserves relics of San Camillo de Lellis in the room where he died. Half his heart is there (the other half being broken up among other brotherhoods of his order), a finger, a gouty foot, death-mask, shoes, clothes.

Often relics are invisible, but there have been notable exceptions, such as the Roman Catholic Pavilion at the Paris Exhibition of 1931 where a *Salle des Martyres* was panelled with big bad paintings of the nastiest deaths, alternating with cartouches framing the vest, or waist-coat, or pale blue satin coat of the holy blessed, to show the haphazard rusty blood and the rent.

German and Austrian baroque and rococo churches were not designed

Left. Cut-paper memorial silhouette. England, nineteenth century. *Above.* Mementoes of Willie Boy (see page 253). United States, twentieth century

Reliquary of a saint at Oberammergau. Germany, early eighteenth century

237

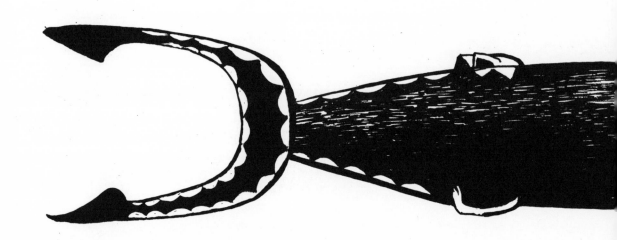

Reliquary in the form of a fish to hold the skull of an ancestor. Wood, carved and painted.
Solomon Islands

for the blood but to enshrine the bones, for choice complete. Banz, for instance, has Saints Valerius, Vercingetorex, Benedictus and Felix, all most beautifully displayed; but few churches have more than one saint. The skeletons are in glass-fronted cases, dressed in Roman armour as envisaged in the early eighteenth century, with short velvet or brocade tunics under embossed leather. They may be standing, or lying on velvet mattresses with thick wedge-shaped cushions, or propped on an elbow with a bone hand under the skull, but the pose is always as fluidly baroque as possible, with perhaps gold lilies or a spray of palm. The thin arm and leg bones may be given weight with cross-garterings of gold ribbon, or are covered tightly with brocade and twisted with gold leaves and pearl flowers; large rosettes emphasize the wrists and sometimes small ones are at the joints of the bare finger bones, which wear rings. The skulls are veiled with gold-edged tulle (there is much gold lace everywhere) and may wear a mitre or a plumed helmet. On the feet are brocade shoes with stamped velvet soles and high polished heels.

In Spain the bone-baroqueries were thick with gold from the Americas. San Juan di Dios in Granada has a fine fairground interior, embellished with plastic gladioli. A holy mole beckons one to the sepulchre up tiny rococo stairs behind the altar, through a long room painted with swinging parrots, into an anteroom with a terrible head of St John Baptist on a charger. An inspection lamp enables one to inspect it, throwing up every pore of the green face, open mouth, contorted tongue, slit eyes (lamp up, closed – lamp down, rolled up in agony, the mole demonstrates happily). In the next room, the shrine is silver in a gold, polished gold, gold, mirror room. Every supporting column is broken into mirror scrolls and cartouches enclosing portraits or bones, and dozens of glass sarcophagi hold jumbles of bones. Huge doors painted with popes and kings can be opened onto the church, so that the shrine is visible high behind the altar, and in a niche behind it is a sham skeleton of another saint, dressed in gauze. The visitor stands like the relics, in gold. The highlights change with every step, hot round the cool pool of silver in the centre. The only colours are those on the doors, a painted dome, and blue ribbon bows on the bones.

In Portugal more bones are used and less gold. The church of Madre de Deus in Lisbon has three stars for good church; it has a faint country-house atmosphere allied to marvellous complications of richness, plan, and levels, an exquisite sacristy, two cloisters, gold, blue tiles, cat-and-

Relics in the upper choir, church of Madre de Deus, Lisbon

Above. More relics from Madre de Deus. *Right.* Reliquary for the arm and hand bones of
St Thomas-à-Becket. Burgos, Spain

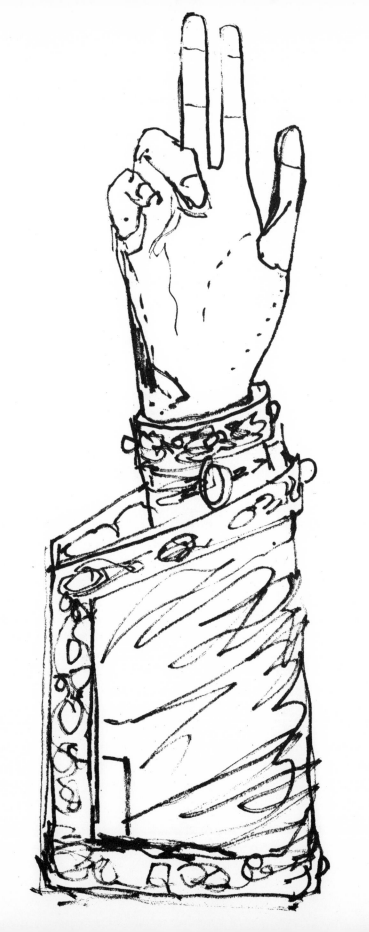

mouse tiles, a flaming urn eight feet high, and superb doors and floors. The upper choir is sombre; the top half of the walls and the whole ceiling are entirely covered with pictures in heavy baroque frames, and between the lowest pictures and the choir stalls run reliquaries in baroque frames and mountings of most loving variation. There are portrait busts with relics framed on their breasts, a bishop, two children, a negro, a skull with crossed bones crowned with shell flowers, a child's skull painted red, a wisp of hair with flanking arms, small bones in settings of rolled and gilded paper.

The church of St Roque (no stars) two miles away has a different technique. On each side of the high altar rises a tall glazed arched recess in which the relics tower up behind glass on shallow shelves, gents on the left (a forest of arms), ladies on the right (fewer arms, more heads).

The anthropomorphic reliquaries made of metals – silver arms and golden heads – are the most beautiful of all, withdrawn and cool. They are widespread through Europe in the treasuries of rich churches, and the saints inside are often far from home – the bones of a really popular saint like Thomas-à-Becket were in great demand and widely distributed. For at least six hundred years reliquary-making was a specialist trade with techniques of its own, some of which survive in the work of church-image makers in Mexico. New techniques in the working of gold, silver, wood, cloth and paper were adapted to the specific display of bones, and the specialists failed in only one thing – the cases were rarely air-tight, and the frames often show brown bones and dusty lace, a mortal ashiness that the makers did not intend.

There are always sporadic attempts at keeping corpses.[1] One of the most famous is that of Jeremy Bentham, who intended himself as a relic. Londoners hear curious reports of him, mummified, green, ghastly, in a glass case in the dining-room at University College. He is there, but different; Bentham's skeleton seated in his own clothes with a superb panama hat on a fine wax portrait head. The only green is the faded black of his coat, and his case, with doors closed, is out in the hall. Bentham wrote in *Auto-Icon* that 'the human body when dissected instead of being an object of disgust is as much more beautiful than any other piece of mechanism as it is more curious and wonderful'. He left his body to his friend and physician Southwood Smith, with instructions for the dissection and exact disposition of his body in a box as an Auto-Icon, with clothes, hat, stick, and entrails, and added: 'If it should so happen that my personal friends and other Disciples should be disposed to meet together . . . for the purpose of commemorating the Founder of the greatest happiness system of morals and legislation my executor will from time to time cause to be conveyed to the room in which they meet the said Box or case with the contents there to be stationed in such part of the room as to the assembled company shall seem meet. . . .' The head was to be treated 'after the manner of the New Zealanders', and Southwood Smith did indeed draw away the fluids 'by placing it under an air-pump over sulphuric acid . . . but all expression was of course gone'. Glass eyes were put in, but it was hopeless, and a wax portrait had to be used for the Auto-Icon, and the skull placed between the feet. It is now in a box, rightly invisible. Tattooing and long practice had helped the New Zealanders.

Jeremy Bentham

There are fewer souvenirs of the deaths of kings than of their coronations (perhaps few kings fulfil their early promise), but a number of locks of Charles I's hair remain, and a last nightcap at Carisbrooke Castle. Odd things survive; someone kept a candle under a glass shade with a card: 'This Candle was one of upward of 700 used at the Lying-in-State in Chelsea Hospital from the 11th to 17th of November 1852 of the Great Duke of Wellington. It was placed in a Candelabra near the foot of the Coffin where it was exposed to great draught and heat.'

As well as relics of the good and great and bad, people like to keep mementos of dead people they loved, and unless tabus have specifically prevented it, the custom has always been widespread. Whole suites of rooms complete with clothes and possessions have been kept 'just as it was the day she died',[2] but the usual mementos have been smaller. They can be either the possessions of the dead, or a bone or hair given as a personal relic, or specially made things prepared for the occasion – mourning clothes, gloves, cards, cakes (wrapped in white paper sealed with black), and jewellery. For centuries in England gloves were given to every mourner at a funeral, kid or cotton according to his social standing, and during the nineteenth century there were little books at the church, padded crushed morocco or cloth with In Memoriam on the cover and the Service for the Burial of the Dead inside, printed with the name and dates of the deceased. Many people had large collections of them.

Jewellery is a good memento; it is personal but does not absorb personality like clothes, and it is beautiful, small and valuable. The best jewellery made specially for mourning is made mostly of gold, enamel, pearls, and the hair of the dead, and is some of the most beautiful jewellery of the eighteenth and nineteenth centuries.

Hair has always been magic; the hair of an enemy burnt to give power, combings saved carefully in little boxes, hair cut off or torn out to be thrown into the grave: hair is very personal, and a good barber will always sweep up the clippings of the previous customer before he starts on ours – we do not like to see them mingled. In the eighteenth century, hair was the medium for several minor arts, as thread for embroidery, twisted on fine wire to make flowers, and plaited for jewellery; it was used with great skill in its muted range of warm and ashy colours. By the middle of the nineteenth century whole parures of hair jewellery were made in large quantities, but I have never seen a memorial parure;

Mourning ring; gold, hair, and rubies. England, late eighteenth century[5]

probably it was felt irreverent to cut off so much hair, and many of the brooches and rings had standard plaits ready round the outside and the hair of the deceased was only put into a little shrine in the middle.

There was also mourning jewellery made only of gold or silver and enamel – there are many simple rings to be found with initials and dates on a band of rich blue enamel; and, oldest and most enduring pattern of all, gold or silver rings with clasped hands or a skull. Jet was used a great deal in the nineteenth century, it was light to wear, took a high polish and was very cheap. Ivory was carved in lamenting patterns and enclosed in glass and ormolu.

The jewellery follows the fashions of its time, so we get skulls from the seventeenth century, temples from the eighteenth, urns and willows from the early nineteenth, ostrich-like plumes later, and debased baroque from the early twentieth. Now nothing.

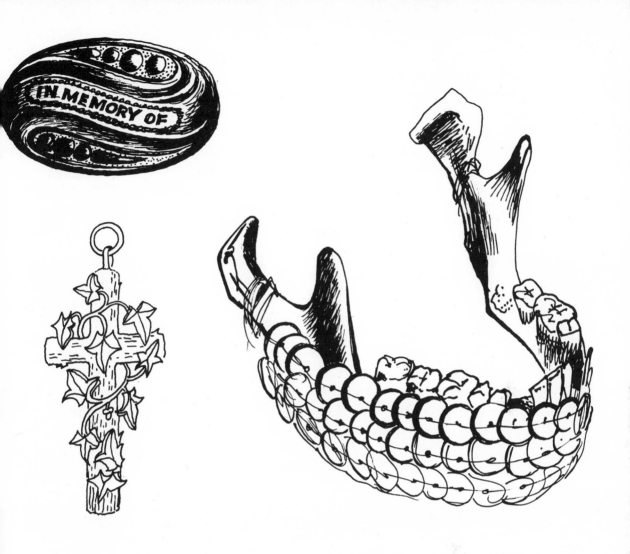

During the middle ages, beautiful painted panels and scrolls were made of royal or special funerals and by Tudor times the arrangement and technique of these had clearly been stylized by artists who specialized in records of state occasions. Later, engravings were made and sold to the general public;[3] at first they were expensive, pasted into long strips, coloured by hand and zig-zagged into an embossed and gilt case. Later they were lithographed and by World War I were line-blocked and not always in colour. They miraculously kept a lot of vigour but ended finally as small scrolls that pulled out of tin cylinders with gilt caps and were wound back again with small handles. Probably, as most of the

Left. Mourning jewellery, including the necklace of teeth mentioned on page 280. Brooches sometimes swivelled to show a portrait or another curl. England, nineteenth century. *Above, left*. Jet brooch and ivory cross. England, nineteenth century. *Right*. Jaw of deceased, decorated with shell, worn as a bracelet or necklace. Papua

processions were military, they were stock for coronations and funerals alike with a different block put in for coach, hearse or gun carriage.

Mass-production multiplied souvenirs till every public occasion was aflutter with paper and ribbons, cheap ephemera sold in the streets. As well as the procession panoramas, funerals had portrait buttons set in black rosettes, flags with black bows, black streamers for children to wave, memorial cards, and, in London at least, paper napkins. These were the ordinary flimsy crêpe-paper or tissue napkins with their variety of brilliant corners and borders, overprinted with portraits, odes and messages for every procession and celebration, price one penny. For funerals, there were heavy black lines, but the napkins were still coloured. China was popular; there were mugs, plates and little dishes with portraits enclosed in black wreaths, and, for the death of Victoria, Goss china came out in the shape of her first shoe. Handkerchiefs with black borders and portraits were made in every material from silk to calico, and there were portraits in every kind of frame, silver through tin to stamped paper. Now, nothing again; for the funeral of Sir Winston Churchill, only programmes; not so much as a kewpie doll with black hair.

Death masks are the most solemn souvenirs, and have been made since man discovered moulding. The Romans used them for the funeral itself but they have usually been made purely as a souvenir, to recall the face of a loved one, and when the process is fashionable and the techniques therefore developed, they can be disturbingly lifelike, but they can also look disturbingly dead. The face is masked and oiled, with special attention to the hairs, and then plaster or some other quick-setting substance is carefully poured over it, including as much as possible of the neck and ears. The dry mould is lifted off, and casts can be made from it. Wax is often used because it looks a little like skin and can be worked over afterwards. The eyes may be left open when the mould is made and then cut away and replaced from the back with bright glass ones. The face can be painted and given false eyelashes, brows and hair. It will always be fragile, and is best kept in a glass case. Life-casts can be made in the same way, but always with the eyes shut and breathing tubes in the nostrils, so they usually look scared stiff.

Casts of very beautiful hands and feet were occasionally made in the eighteenth and nineteenth centuries (a hand can look very well on a velvet cushion), and there are accounts of whole waxworks sitting in drawingrooms but I have never seen any. Madame Tussaud's has a few

Memorial rosette sold in the streets at the funeral of George Vth. Photograph on celluloid, and cloth. England, 1936

SOUVENIR

IN COMMEMORATION OF

HYDE PARK SHRINE.

···∘○○∘···

The Shrine is immediately facing the people as they go in the Marble Arch entrance to Hyde Park.

The public will be able to lay flowers on the Shrine from Two o'clock until Seven o'clock on Sunday, and to see the flowers on the Shrine during the Bank Holiday.

REMEMBRANCE DAY

AUGUST 4, 1918.

MEMBERS OF THE LONDON VOLUNTEERS

will guard the Shrine.

death masks in the collection;[4] and of course the Chamber of Horrors is a rich gallery of souvenirs of death; a baby-farmer's perambulator, the actual clothes of some of the murderers, and haunting dim photographs of the Bungalow on the Crumbles near Eastbourne, where Patrick Mahon cut up and boiled Emily Kaye in saucepans trying to get rid of the body.[5]

Relics of famous criminals used to be as popular as those of the saints, and stardom as haphazardly given. For instance, no special glamour surrounded the life of Willie Boy, an outlaw and a baddy, hunted down by goodies in the finest tradition of the American West in 1909. He shot himself when near capture, gun barrel to chest, one shoe off, big toe on trigger. The posse, which included a Ben de Crevecoeur, found his bloated body in a blood-caked white shirt, and bravely fired several hundred rounds till the hills rang. A newspaperman called Madison took photographs of them all standing round Willie and then a bonfire was suggested so they collected brushwood, and took souvenirs, buttons from the nasty shirt, and the loose shoe, while the sheriff had the bullet to engrave for a watch-fob. In 1958 the ashes of the fire were searched and the metal parts of Willie Boy's braces and remaining shoe were found, and photographed, and reproduced in a book, and are probably kept in a small cardboard box to this day. Criminals' relics do not seem ever to have been so richly boxed as saints' relics, unless enough people were killed for murder to become war, when again there are shrines. There is a good shrine in the monastery at Batalha in Portugal, the Museum of Allied Combatants in the refectory. Four great screens, in heaviest gothic-pinnacled wooden frames, are painted white, and on them are fixed bronze mementoes; laurel-wreaths, palms, sprays, plaques and helmets from all the allies. Underneath one frame is a little cluster of tins and plastic bottles of oil, offerings for the lamp burning on the grave of two unknown soldiers in another chapel. Cases hold battle honours, more bronze trophies, a boy-scout offering with a lacquered scouts hat, and hundreds of silk ribbons, gold lettered, in all the allied colours, from old wreaths. All is *la gloire*; some old shell-cases holding up guard ropes came as quite a shock.

Left. Ancestor-figure in the form of a turkey, carved wood, 11·4 in. high. From the altar of a chief's mother. Benin, Africa, late nineteenth century. *Right.* Memorial gift from a chief mourner at a Bakuba funeral, just under actual size. These were made of powdered red camwood (the currency), mixed with gum, hardened and carved. Africa, late nineteenth century

255

WHERE DEATH GETS YOU

Where death gets you
Down

Where death gets you
Into the caretaker's room of a Waiting Mortuary, Munich.

At the beginning of the twentieth century, Munich had ten Waiting Mortuaries. The corpses were laid out in two immense rooms at the North Mortuary with lace, chiffon, hot-house flowers and large numbered tickets. At the head of each coffin stood an ornamental metal-work gibbet holding up a cord. One end was connected to a bell and the other to a ring which was placed on a finger of the corpse so that the least movement would ring the bell: 'The relative purity of the atmosphere is really astonishing. There is a room for the rich and another for the poor, adjoining each other. Nothing distinguishes them, except perhaps the quality of the flowers provided for the respective classes ... Between the two mortuaries is the caretaker's room – a narrow cell, containing the

Left. The caretaker in a Waiting Mortuary, Munich. Germany, late nineteenth century.
Above. Albatross bill mounted with a spring to make a clip for letters, or bills. England, late nineteenth century

bell aparatus, which is enclosed in a long cupboard, like the case of a grandfather's clock. For furniture – a table, a chair, and a couch. Windows look into the mortuary. It is here that the caretaker passes the greater part of his existence. He has to make frequent rounds of inspection, and is not allowed to leave under any pretext whatever, no matter for how short a time, unless he leaves a substitute. In the evening he stretches himself upon his couch, where the slightest tinkle of the bell would arouse him. This frequently happens; the warning bell is so sensitive that the least shake of the corpse sets it in motion. But the guardian is not at all flustered; various causes may agitate the bell, and the waking of a corpse is a very rare occurrence. Nevertheless, the caretaker goes to ascertain the cause of the alarm and, having assured himself that the corpse preserves all the signs of death, he readjusts the cord, and returns to continue his sleep.'[1]

Where death gets you
Inventing

Anthony de Chionski, a retired Polish parson living in Dresden, put a mouse in a retort and sucked out the air, so that 'the mouse, which for want of air in the meantime has been choked, is more and more swolling till it bursts'. He argued from this that the same would happen to a human corpse, so he invented an apparatus to check death. It looked like a covered bath on wheels with a pump at the end and comfortable steps for the operator. At the head end was a window in the lid through which a second operator watched for the movement which de Chionski was sure would occur if life were not extinct. At the first movement, pumping stops, and the lid is whipped off. If there is no movement, dead for sure after fifteen minutes.[2]

Where death gets you
Worried

Count Karnicé-Karnicki, Chamberlain to the Czar, Doctor of Law of

Louvain University, went to the funeral of a young Belgian girl who came out of a trance as the earth fell on the coffin. Her screams upset him, and he set out to find a sure way of preventing such tragedies. His answer was an hermetically sealed coffin with a long tube about three and a half inches in diameter fixed in the lid above the breast of the corpse, where a glass ball was set, attached to a spring which communicated up through the tube to a box on top of it, some feet above ground level. The slightest movement of the chest wall would stir the globe and release the spring, whereupon the lid of the box would fly open, letting light and air into the coffin, a flag would spring up, a bell ring for half an hour, a lamp burn after sunset and the tube magnify the voice inside. Estimated cost, 13s.[3]

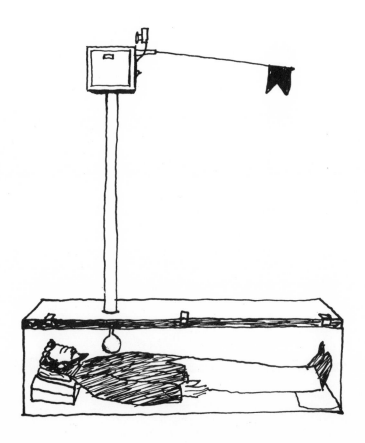

Above. Count Karnicé-Karnicki's apparatus set ready. *Next page.* The apparatus at work. France, late nineteenth century

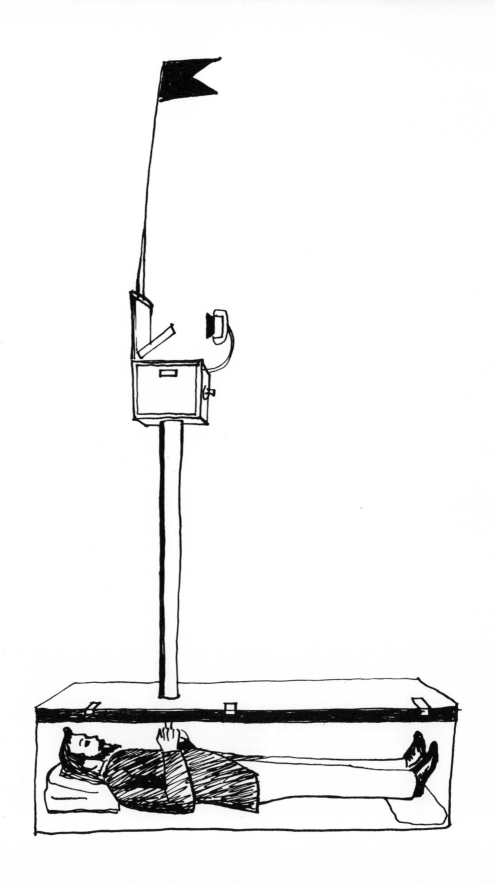

Where death gets you
Sin-eating

Paid mourners (watchers, wailers, mimes, mutes) have a long and widespread history, and there have often been rites and prayers to help free
the dead from punishment, but in Britain, especially Wales, sin-eating
by a paid individual continued into the nineteenth century. The sin-eater
was an outcast who took upon himself the sins of the dead. Bread and
beer and sixpence were handed to him across the corpse and he ate and
drank and went away and the platter and beaker were burned.

Where death gets you
Kissing the dead hand

In 1355 the King of Portugal took against Inez de Castro, a beautiful
Spaniard who lived at Coimbra and was either the wife or mistress of his
son Pedro. She refused to go back to Spain and the King had her beheaded.
Pedro rose against his father and took the throne, and then settled down
for revenge. Two of the executioners were caught and their hearts cut
out, one from the front, one from the back. Pedro had the hearts taken to
the banqueting hall and tried to eat them, but he couldn't, and had them
burnt. In April 1361 he had Inez dug up and enthroned beside him, and
proclaimed her Queen, and all his courtiers lined up to kiss her hand.

Where death gets you
To the Cabaret du Néant, Paris, 1920

Oswell Blakeston has described to me how one was welcomed by a man
dressed as an undertaker with 'Come in, coffin worm! A brother is dead.'
He took one into the *Salle d'Intoxication,* furnished with coffins on
trestles. From the ceiling hung a candelabra made of skulls of different
sizes and the visitor was told they came from one person at different
ages. Tapers were lighted and the undertaker intoned 'Behold the
microbes of death! Drink them with resignation.' The master of cere-

CABARET du NÉANT - Paris-Montmartre — n° 1. Salle d'Intoxication

CABARET du NÉANT - Paris-Montmartre — no5, 3ᵉ Caveau. Les Spectres tristes

Above. Souvenir postcards of the Cabaret du Néant
Right. Two of Haden's inventions for speedier, more hygienic decay; the basket, and the 'Earth to Earth' coffin used by the London Necropolis Co. (see page 173), made of a fast-rotting material, probably 'stout paste-board'. The baskets are known to have been in use until 1928, possibly later. England, nineteenth century

monies held up a thigh-bone and told grim stories. Attention was drawn to some large paintings of dancers at the old Moulin Rouge, and lights were switched on behind these pictures, and the figures changed to skeletons. Then one was led through dark and narrow passages to the *Caveau des Trépassés*. Here one of the visitors was induced to step into a coffin. A sheet was thrown over him, and then, with the help of mirrors, he was seen to decompose and become a skeleton. After this, the party was led through more dark and narrow passages into the third cave, where *les spectres tristes* were produced. Lastly, a lady was coerced into sitting in a chair on a small stage. Her outer garments seemed to vanish and then she appeared to indulge in what the programme called 'many odd practices'.

Where death gets you
Into a duke's garden

During the summer of 1875, the Duke of Sutherland invited the nobility and gentry of London to a garden party to secure their attention to an improved system of wickerwork coffins devised by Mr Seymour Haden to speed up decomposition. 'During two days everybody accepted His Grace's invitation with alacrity, for everybody does not often get invited to a ducal residence. Everybody read a neatly printed circular, poked in his hand on passing the door, and then everybody, after entering the aristocratic precincts of Stafford House, was permitted to moralize *ad lib* over a heap of oblong baskets displayed upon the grass.' The corpse was put into a deal box with holes bored in it and the box packed with moss was put into the basket.[4]

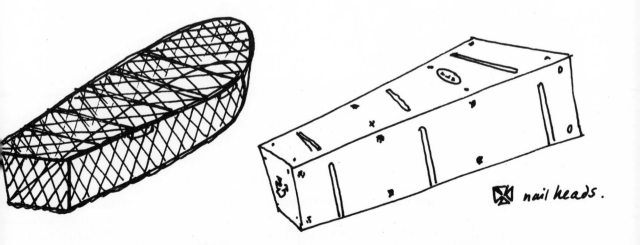

nail heads.

Where death gets you
Dressed up as a skeleton

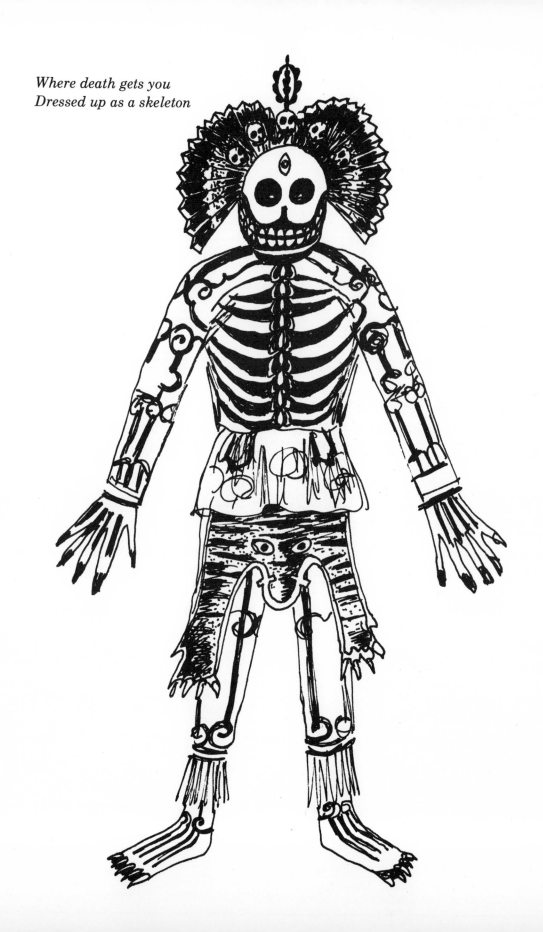

Where death gets you
Trying to think of a better name for scent than 'Ashes of Roses'

Where death gets you
Finishing the Ashanti Kings, 1895

The Ashanti, like many other people, never admitted that anyone died –
he was visiting relations or had gone to live somewhere else – but nevertheless they took great pains to see that creature comforts were prepared
for the dead, especially kings.

The corpse was washed and dressed, and at each stage an attendant
was killed so that the dead man would always have someone around to
hand him water, a towel, robes, and the beautiful golden ornaments. At
night, the king was taken to the death-room in the palace, with some of
his wives dressed in white, and wearing gold. They got drunk, and were
strangled, and servants for every kind of duty were killed too. This went
on for several days, while the corpse stayed in the palace, and then it
was carried to the dripping-place and lay dripping in a perforated coffin
for eighty days and nights. The bones were then scraped and oiled and
articulated with gold wire, complete but changed to fit a small coffin as
long as the thigh bones – these coffins were covered with fabric, green
silk or black velvet, and decorated with gold roundels.

A year after the death, the coffin was taken to the mausoleum in
Tantama, where it had a room of its own and an entourage of live wives
and cooks, replaced when they died. There were eight kings at Tantama,
but when Baden-Powell arrived the bones and gold had all been got
away: 'Then, in accordance with orders, we set the whole fetish village
in flames, and a splendid blaze it made.'[5]

Where death gets you
Around London

Mrs Basil Holmes went to every burial ground, yard, and old plague pit
in London, asking, walking, climbing fences, never deterred. She wrote

Devil-dance costume. Tibet, twentieth century

an excellent book describing them all and adding sound advice: 'An appearance of utter insignificance and an air of knowing where you are going and what you want, is the passport for all parts of London.'[6]

Where death gets you
Keeping your tobacco in a skull

> *Never laugh when a ghost goes by –*
> *It may be your turn next to die.*
> *They wrap you up in a big white sheet*
> *And throw you down, six feet deep.*
> *All goes well for a week or two,*
> *Then things start happening; all is new.*
>
> *Worms crawl in and worms crawl out,*
> *And ants play ping-pong on your snout*
> *One worm that's not quite so shy*
> *Crawls in one ear and out one eye,*
> *Till your blood turns to a sickery green*
> *And oozes out like Devonshire cream.*

Anonymous, twentieth century

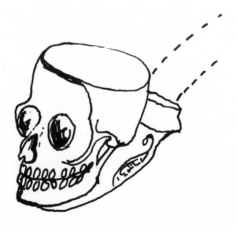

Above. Bowl of clay pipe with green glass eyes, made by Gambier, Paris, and used by medical students. *Right.* Carved wooden tobacco-jar, provenance unknown. Both nineteenth century

Where death gets you
Doing something really worth while about taxidermy

Not everyone is satisfied with just stuffing animals or skinning them and then keeping them about the place plain. Some men have seen them as the materials for *tableaux-morts,* groups of small animals stuffed on their hind legs, dressed and posed as people. They are getting rare, partly because fewer people learn the skills – small animals are obviously difficult to stuff – but kittens, always appealing in life, are irresistible in death to *tableaux*-makers. I have seen a series of large glass cases setting out the history of the three little kittens who lost their mittens, with a series of matching tabby mothers, and multiple sets of ginger, tortoiseshell

The Kittens' Wedding, Bramber Museum, Sussex. Mid-nineteenth century

A standard lamp supported by a stuffed emu. England, late nineteenth century

and black kits bewailing their tiny crocheted mittens with awful little tightly stitched-up mouths. The *tableaux* are also getting rare because they are decaying; conditions were rarely sterile, and other, smaller, animals are beginning to win. Potter's Museum at Bramber in Sussex has an excellent collection. Walter Potter (1835–1918) was an enthusiastic taxidermist who was inspired by a sister's book of nursery rhymes; the Death and Burial of Cock Robin would, he saw, absorb many of his specimens. The group of nearly a hundred birds was finished in 1861 and is still in the museum with *tableaux* of The Babes in the Wood, the Kittens' Tea and Croquet Party (37 kits), the Upper Ten (21 red squirrels at their club), the Lower Five (15 rats in a den), Rabbits' Village School (48 little scholars), The House that Jack Built, The Guinea Pigs' Cricket Match (observe two spectators in the refreshment marquee evidently more interested in each other than in the match), and Kittens' Wedding (note the expressions). There are a lot of curios (mummy's hand 4,000 years old, Russian black bread 1854), many animals and birds, and the local freaks (kittens with seven legs and two tails, or three eyes and two mouths, a young duck with four legs, four wings, three eyes, two tails and double beak, and three moles, all unusual in colour), Doré drawings, and a mounted cabbage stalk from Jersey. Something for everybody.

Henry Jones' Musée Phusée Glyptic at Stratford-on-Avon was a collection of representational sculptures made from the roots of trees and other natural objects. Phusiglyptic sculpture was partly nature and partly art, excogitated by contemplation of the roots. The museum must have been broken up years ago, but there is a splendid account of it with drawings of a lot of the exhibits. Among them is a horse's vertebra painted probably a century earlier to represent a parson preaching with upraised arms, and it or one very like it, survives; bones preferred to roots.[7]

During the 1860s whole stuffed grouse and pheasants were worn as ladies' hats, then tiger and bear claws were made into jewellery, then the hoofs of favourite horses were made into inkstands; by 1896 bears held card trays in the hall, and almost anything might be a chair or stool, an elephant sitting up like a cat made a horrid hall-porter's chair, monkeys held up lamps, albatross beaks clipped letters, elephants' feet holding whisky bottles were commonplace enough to be a registered design, an ostrich leg made a door-stop, and Sir Edwin Landseer had designed an antler hat-stand and an otter chair.

The vertebra of a horse painted to represent a parson

Where death gets you
Obeying Father

In 1817, John Snart published *Thesaurus of Horror*, a book explaining the various ways in which premature burial may be avoided. 'The test or method used by the Turkish physicians seems very simple and natural, for they never think a subject dead, or even *hopeless,* while there is any irritability or contractile power in the *sphincter ani*; this may be easily performed by taking an ox, or a large pig's bladder, with a tube attached to its orifice, and inflating it in the usual way, by blowing air into it from the mouth, after which (if it be cold weather) it may be moderately heated by immersion in hot water, or holding it before a fire, and its tube inserted into one corner of the mouth, the air may be forced down the throat by compressing the bladder, while an assistant closely stops the nose and lips, except the aperture which admits the tube, it will soon be ascertained whether there be a thorough passage for the escapement of the air, or whether any muscular action takes place in its efforts to pass.

'It is scarcely requisite to say, that the subject (for *obvious* reasons) should not be laid on a *bed*, or any other *soft* substance, while this experiment is made, though it is indispensable that they should be in a *Prostrate* situation. This appears so simple a test, that it ought never to be omitted, even if all other trials had failed, and it is within everyone's power to try it.'

Mr Snart, who cannot have known about M. Josat who won first prize from the Académie de France for the invention of an even simpler apparatus – clawed forceps for pinching the nipples of the corpse – suggested many other methods: keeping the corpse warm under close watch for at least a week, with no indecent experiments for twenty-four hours except holding a looking-glass to the mouth or brushing the soles of the feet with strong pickle; or electricity; or warm baths; or pasting tissue-paper over the mouth and nose; or blowing Scotch snuff up the nose; or pouring volatile tincture of ammonia down the throat with a funnel. If none of these seem conclusive, he says, cut the jugulars, or separate the carotid arteries, divide the medulla, or pierce the heart.

The author gave a copy of the book to his daughter with an Injunction: 'Remember that when you received this Book from the hands of your Father, who wrote it for the benefit of the *whole world*! It was under the most solemn assurance of faithfully discharging all the various obligations of it towards him, in that *awful* period when (should you survive him) Your fidelity will be put to the utmost test!

'And upon the discharge of this paramount duty *alone* depends his future Blessing & your Welfare! For by the laws of Nature, which are irrevocable; Reward attaches to Virtue and Obedience, But Punishment and unavailing Remorse to Disobedience! And dreadful would it be to reflect That you had violated your father's dying injunction

Signed under the unequivocally
Solemn Engagement of full obedience

to the extent   this 17th day of August 1817'
of my power

She signed it Neariah Snart with an understandably trembling hand.

Where death gets you
Keeping your toothpowder in a coffin

Hayden Coffin was an actor who sold toothpowder in a nice turquoise blue mummy-case made of pottery. Wrapped round it was a turquoise blue booklet explaining that the powder was based on a valuable prescription of his father, the late Dr C. R. Coffin.

A Discovery by

HAYDEN COFFIN

THAT'S PATENTED

Dr Coffin like all leading practitioners, wrote many prescriptions, and among these [Hayden Coffin discovered] a most valuable one for TOOTH POWDER, which is now used as a basis for the most *perfect, efficacious,* and *economical* dentifrice before the public . . . germicide, thoroughly antiseptic . . . absolutely novel . . .

Use the H. C. BRUSH-A-BIT

It being essential to have a strong container into which the powder could be compressed *direct*, and also easily distinguishable from the stereotyped Tooth Powder Box, or Paste Tube, the historic figure of the USHABTI as adapted 'Answers' the practical purpose

Ushabti Tooth Powder will ANSWER

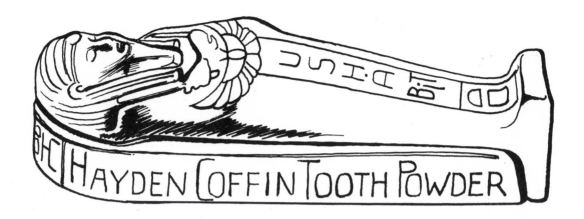

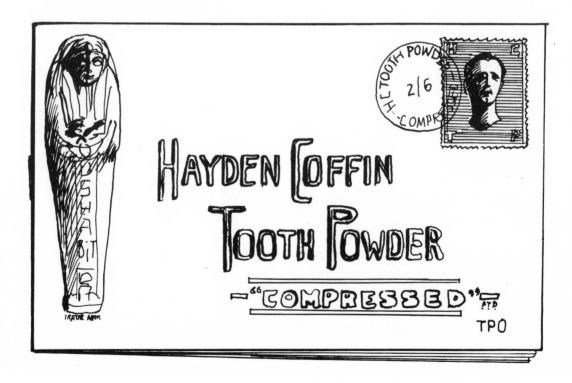

Where death gets you
Up

James M. O'Kelley, of New York, invented penny-in-the-slot machines. In 1901, accounts were published of his new invention, the Navohi, for burial in the air because the earth, with an estimated ten corpses per square foot of surface, was getting overcrowded. The Navohi was an elliptical structure like a big egg-shell with a smaller one inside. It was made of silk with three silk wings attached to the lower sides, and the enclosed cavity was filled with 'ordinary illuminating gas' under pressure. The coffin was thickly walled inside with wax and furnished with a valve. At the last moment it was filled with acid to cover the corpse, sealed, and put upright into the Navohi, resting on a rubber cushion which then contracted half-an-inch. In the middle of the cushion was 'a rough pin working through an inflammable composition'. The acid ate the flesh and made gases which escaped through the valve, the coffin weighed less, the cushion rose, the rough pin was pulled through the inflammable composition and started a fire. Air poured in, made a gas-balloon, and the corpse was rushed flaming like a rocket into the sky, trailing graceful clouds of white vapour. An illustration shows the funeral party waving goodbye from the roof, and there is a less-than-explanatory section through the balloon; the inventor must have feared infringements of patent, as he had already sent a cat and a large dead dog, up.[8]

IVE BEEN DOING SOME SERIOUS THINKING
A THOUGHT HAS JUST COME INTO MY HEAD
IF YOU DONT HAVE A DRINK WHEN YOU'RE LIVING
YOU'LL HAVE A HELL OF A JOB WHEN YOU'RE DEAD

LOVING DEATH

"YOU'VE HAD IT"

LOVING DEATH

Lovely death. We pick at it as we pick at a scab. Our pleasure in it takes many forms; Justice Shallow sitting in his orchard was simply glad that he had outlived so many friends. Dead! What supreme satisfaction!

But if we have to consider the death of a stranger, we like to see some shape in it; when we read in the newspapers of someone balancing an electric fire cosily on the edge of the bath, knocking it in, and getting electrocuted, the death is just sad or stupid. An ordinary accident will not do, and suicide by its very nature is without tragedy, but occasionally a death occurs in the quest for stronger life which has the inevitability of Oedipus or Lear. A refrigeration engineer in London had a death of this sort. He was found dead in bed in Highgate on a Sunday.[1] The room was full of electric wiring. He himself was wired up, and strapped to him with adhesive bandages was a piece of electrical apparatus shaped and dressed like a woman. Death by misadventure.

The deaths of the Collyer brothers in New York set an almost impossibly high standard; such perfection takes more time and trouble than the average man is prepared to give. The brothers lived in almost complete seclusion in a brownstone house on Upper Fifth Avenue. The elder brother, Langley, was blind and never went out at all; Homer only went

Left. Sugar skull for the Day of the Dead. Mexico, present day. *Above.* Earthenware mug. England, present day

out to get food. On March 21st 1947 the police had an anonymous telephone call stating that someone was dead in the house. They found that all five floors, roof to ground, floor to ceiling, were stacked and jammed with rubbish. Through the hall and up the stairs were narrow precarious tunnels, booby-trapped all the way. The blind Langley was dead in bed on the second floor, ill-clad and thin. Homer could not be found, so for nineteen days the police tunnelled from the basement and down from holes in the roof. They took out more than a hundred tons of newspapers, furniture, pieces of old cars, five violins, seventeen pianos, thousands of cardboard boxes, rags. Homer was found in the same room as his brother, starved to death under one of his own booby traps.

Beyond the enjoyment of the good works of death lies necrophilia. It must be a difficult passion to satisfy; very few people admit to the liberal sentiments of Henri Blot, who dug up an eighteen-year-old ballet dancer at St Ouen in 1886. He got away with that one but was caught with his next corpse. At his trial he said, *'Que voulez-vous? Chacun à son goût, le mien est pour les corps'*.[2] So because it is probably the most carefully concealed of all aberrations there are no publicly known observances or special artefacts for necrophilia.

Provided, though, that it does not become overtly sexual, interest in death is seen to be quite natural, and some of the greatest artists have painted the dead, or used the corpse as a medium, turning it, and particularly the skull, into works of art, as we saw in Chapter One. Professional artists draw death sometimes for their own pleasure, and sometimes to order; noble families sometimes commissioned portraits of their important corpses, and there is an account of a man who in the early nineteenth century employed an artist to paint daily portraits of his beautiful mistress as she died of consumption. Of course Christianity, a religion based on death and suffering, offered in its heyday an enormous choice of deaths – crucifixions (plain, upside down, spreadeagled), wheels, gridirons, stonings, flayings, beheadings, fire and the sword in sickening variety. St Ursula offered 11,001 deaths, and St Sebastian, traditionally beautiful, sex and death together.

Some very elegant things praise death. By Roman times, bones were aesthetically acceptable, and the Renaissance artists returned to them with enthusiasm; Vesalius' beautiful engravings of the human skeleton were widely known and used, and at Schloss Ambras in Austria is an ebony cabinet with a graceful Vesalius-posed skeleton contemplating

Bone chapel, Sao Francisco, Evora. Portugal, *c.* 1600

the Apples of the Hesperides.[3] Holbein put a wonderful *trompe l'oeil* into his painting. The Ambassadors, and the Dance of Death engravings appeared in hundreds of variations. The theme was both moral and amusing. In the earlier versions Death was personified as a skeleton who called the tune to which humans danced. Later the skeleton danced with them, or appeared leering over men's shoulders at moments of joy and triumph; The Dance is very like Dunbar's *Lament for the Makers*.[4]

The late sixteenth and early seventeenth centuries were the zenith of general enjoyment of death; the skull, the clock, and the flight of time darken painting and poetry for a whole century. In the eighteenth century, the earlier Dance of Death theme was picked up again with greater grace, and *squeletteries* were added to *singeries* and *chinoiseries*; skeletons posed as La Veille Coquette, as gardeners, carpenters and field-marshals.

Skulls and bones have not only inspired the arts, they have themselves been used to make them; I have been given a beautiful necklace, ivory beads at first glance, but made of the graduated teeth of a family, pre-served, pierced, and strung – such a pretty thought, each one has been carved into a little skull.[5]

Grand collections have been made by monks of the Roman Catholic church, keeping the Brothers' bones. Some of these were simply stored in ossuaries, but others were used as building materials. There is a most impressive stark chapel in São Francisco at Evora in Portugal, about sixty feet long, where the entire walls and six pillars supporting a trivial painted ceiling are covered with solid, simple bonework. Arm bones retain sharpness in the pillars, pilasters, and some arcading, while skulls are used both to emphasize the main ribs of the ceiling vaults and, with the heads of femurs, as infill on the walls. The altar is routine carved baroque for contrast but over two flanking doors are fine keystones made of pelvises with skulls set slightly askew on them, distinct therefore from the other skulls – lucky Brothers. One other is distinct; his corpse, dried and tattering, short of forearms and feet, hangs on a peg.

'Who is that?'
'A Brother.'
Near him hangs a small something in a straw hood.
'And that?'
'A baby.'
'No, not a baby.'
'No.'

Underneath the church of the Immaculate Conception in Rome lies The Celebrated Cemetery of the Capuchin Fathers, a unique work of art, as the souvenir folder rightly tells us, in an underground passage forty metres long, consisting of a corridor and six arched compartments con-taining the bones of some 4,000 religious who died between 1528 and 1870.

The brother on the wall, Evora. Portugal, *c.* 1600. *Following pages, left.* The catacombs of the Capuchin Fathers, Rome, eighteenth century. *Right.* The ossuary in a church at Kutna Hora, Czechoslovakia

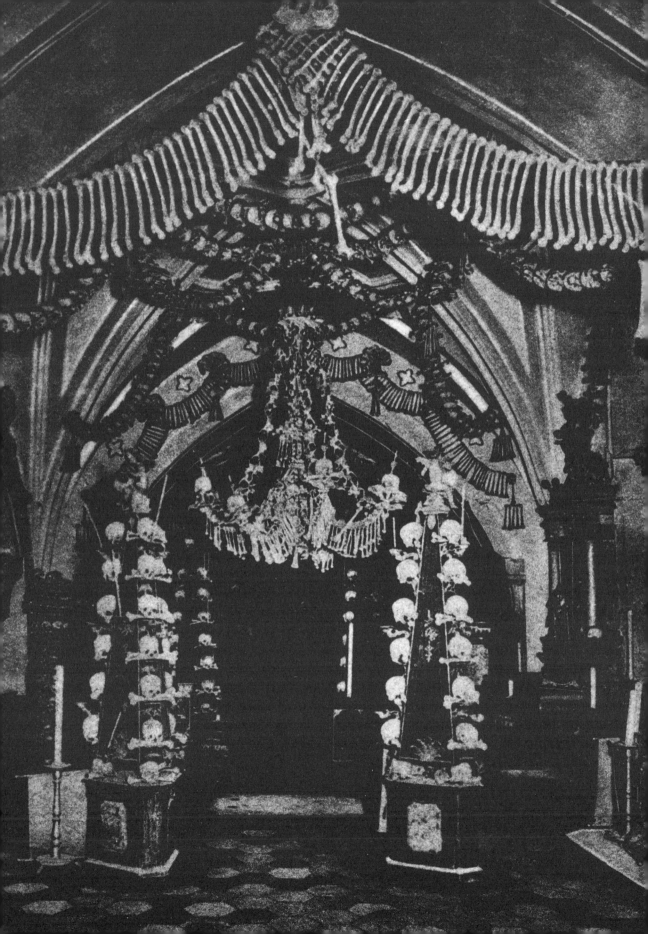

The bones of the Fathers must have been collected in an ossuary for more than two hundred years until the eighteenth century, when tradition says that a French friar designed the work, which was carried out by the living Fathers. The ceiling of the corridor and the vaults are nicely decorated with light baroque decoration in bonework. The main lines of the architecture are emphasized with lines of femur, fibula, tibia, humerus, ulna, and within these limits are curlicues and stars of ribs, vertebri and pelvises finished with the elegant little bones of hands, feet, fingers and toes. Skulls and other bones surplus to requirement on the ceilings line the walls in rich solid dadoes, worked into arches and recesses that frame the whole skeletons or mummies of the specially blessed, who lie and lean and leer, cowled in their habits as they lived, lit by the settled dust.

In Palermo, where there are 8,000 corpses in the catacombs, it was also a privilege of the aristocracy to be treated after death in a particular manner at the Cappuchin Zita Church. The process has been described to me by Aurelio Pappalardo as follows: 'The corpse was seated with no preparation for three days in an enclosed room, at the end of which time all the internal organs had come away. Then for two or three months it was bricked up to desiccate in the dry air and then taken to the Zita where the corpses were put in an enormously high room which has four or five shelves, some lying, some standing, some seated, tied under the arms to stop them falling. Some are skeletons, some retain a little skin, some even have hair and eyes and teeth. They were never laid out or arranged in any way so that the eyes are open and the mouths gape with life. There are fragments of clothes, and each corpse has a name-plate, very legible, round the neck. There is one child that has had some embalming. It is very beautiful and very horrible; people go to look and point out ancestors.'

A most devoted and skilful worker with corpses was the Dutch anatomist Fredrik Ruysch, 1638–1731, who made his own famous museum in Amsterdam. There were hundreds of carefully prepared and beautifully catalogued dissections, and he invented a secret method of embalming which was said to preserve the bloom of life itself, so the museum also had a large collection of peachy corpses. When Ruysch was an old man the collection was bought by Peter the Great and taken to St Petersburg, while Ruysch began a new collection. His masterpieces were the pictures and *tableaux* that he made from organs of the human body.

One of Ruysch's tableaux of anatomical specimens

Plate I.

Tab. I.

A series of them were engraved 'ad vivum C. Huyberts' in 1740. In the one reproduced on the opposite page, there is an hexagonal base on which is piled up what looks like a group of minerals and fossils with branches of coral. It is in fact made of anatomical preparations, heart, liver, glands, all can be identified, and the corals are veins. The elegant trophy is crowned by a child's or a dwarf's skeleton in an attitude of woe, and flanking the base are smaller stands with two more skeletons. One holds up a tiny scythe, which might be a dissecting instrument, and the other weeps into a handkerchief of some veined integument. A skeleton in another *tableau* plays a violin made of arteries and a piece of bone, and there is a picture of a cemetery.[6]

Death triggers off pop as well as fine art – a picture post-card of a skull constructed out of two happy riders on a bobsleigh, an enormous parchment skeleton in the cathedral in Murcia, rows of dancing skeletons in flick-books, or torn from newspaper to amuse theatre queues, plastic skulls and shrunken heads, comic post-cards, human skin for binding books and making lampshades, thousands and thousands of skinned pet animals and trophies of the chase, pottery in the shape of skulls, real skulls for drinking-cups, and – still embracing a whole country for two days every year – Mexico's Dia de los Muertos.

The things for the Day of the Dead may be ephemeral in deliberate symbolism of the quick passing of life, or simply because ephemera are cheap to make. Either way, they are difficult to collect and keep, impossible to illustrate adequately in black and white, made of clay, wire, sugar and thin paper, losing their beauty in storage. Some of them were shown at the Tate Gallery in London in the spring of 1953, and no one who saw it can have forgotten the room full of vermilion, pink, lemon and arsenic-green and white, paper and tin and feathers; the heart lifted, the mind sang, and here lies the uniqueness of the Mexican preoccupation with death – it is lyrical and loving, skull, bird and irony.

On the 1st and 2nd of November, the *calaveras* are circulated; *calavera* means skull, and these are lampoons illustrated with skeletons, natural or clothed or uniformed, going about the business of the living, making love, or working an expresso machine. They are not as well drawn as they were in the nineteenth century – Mexico needs a Gerald Scarfe.

Paper figures, more than life-size and sometimes festooned with fireworks, to hang above the streets on the Day of the Dead. Mexico, present day

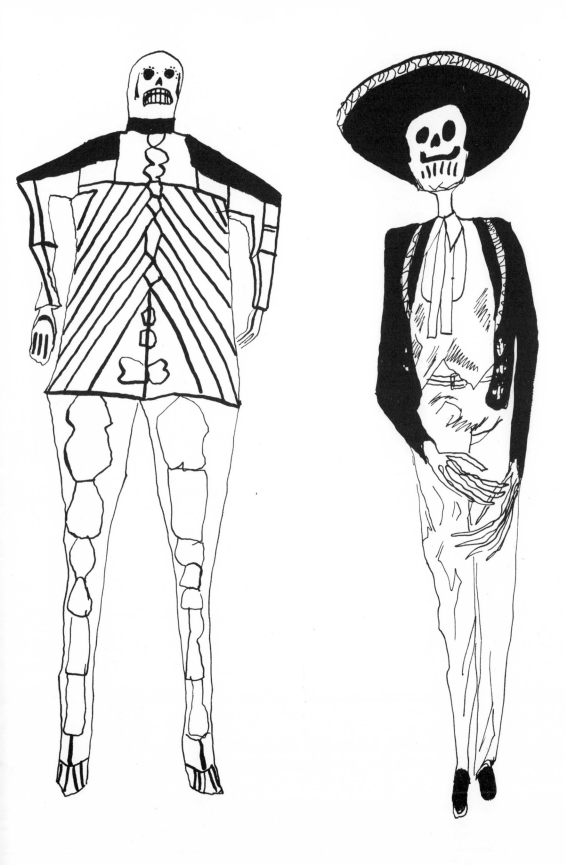

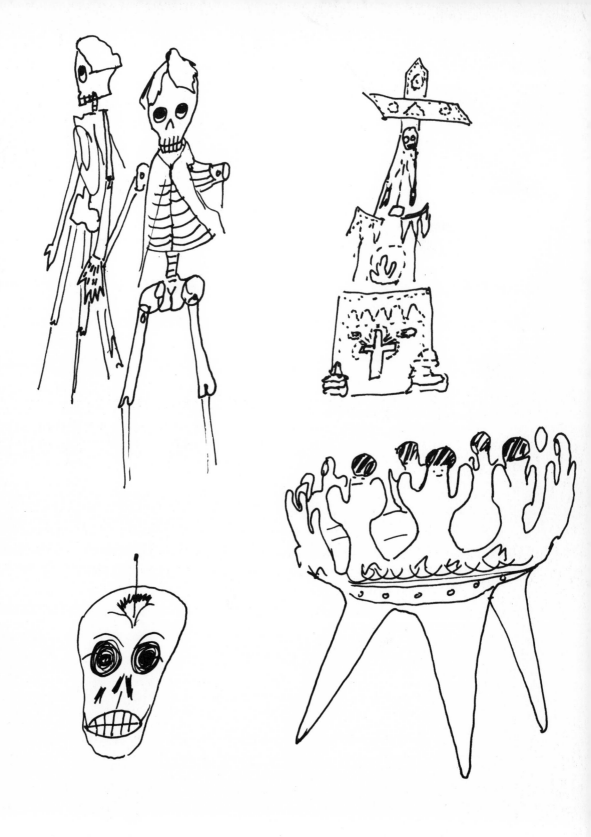

Above. Skeletons, a skull, a cardboard pulpit with skeleton priest, and a candlestick. *Right*. A clay and wire skeleton with a pink paper fan. All for the Day of the Dead. Mexico, present day

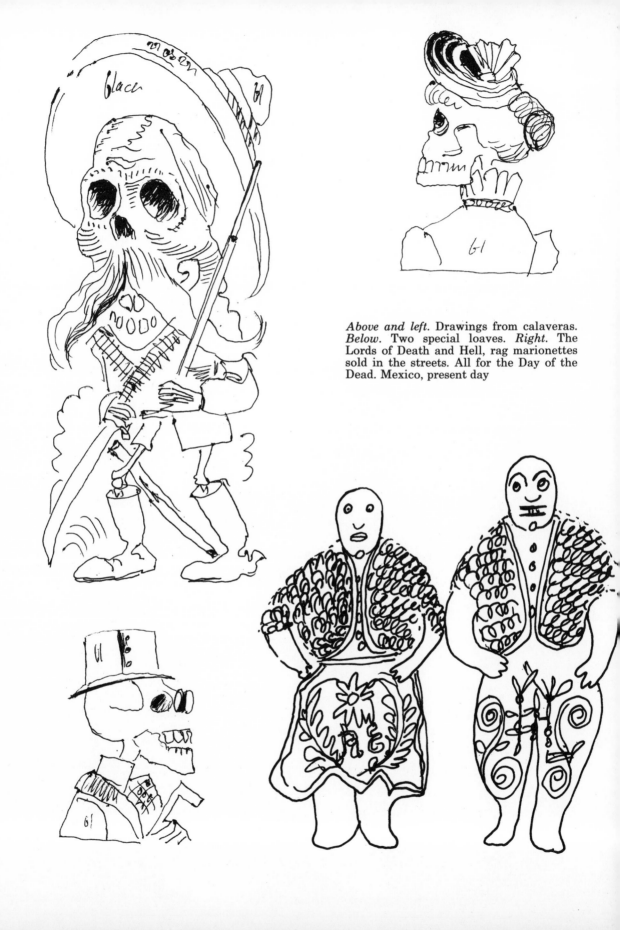

Above and left. Drawings from calaveras. *Below.* Two special loaves. *Right.* The Lords of Death and Hell, rag marionettes sold in the streets. All for the Day of the Dead. Mexico, present day

On November 1st, All Saints Day, special food used to be cooked for the dead, the favourite dishes of the loved ones. Wild duck was specially favoured, and bread baked in the shapes of animals and people. In the evening everyone met and went at midnight to the cemetery, where the women and children sat round the graves, with candles, marigolds, the food, fruit, wine, and household saints set out on top. In the church were presents for the unknown dead. Later, the food was taken home and sensibly eaten. The loving picnics round the graves have now stopped almost everywhere, but bread is still made in special shapes. Next day, the dead are prayed for, and in the evening there may be a performance of *Don Juan* ending with a ballet of skeletons, first complete and then breaking into disjointed bones and skulls.

Lick your love to death. Beatle lollipop; strawberry-pink boiled sugar, with photograph on white paper, diameter 5¾ in. England, 1964

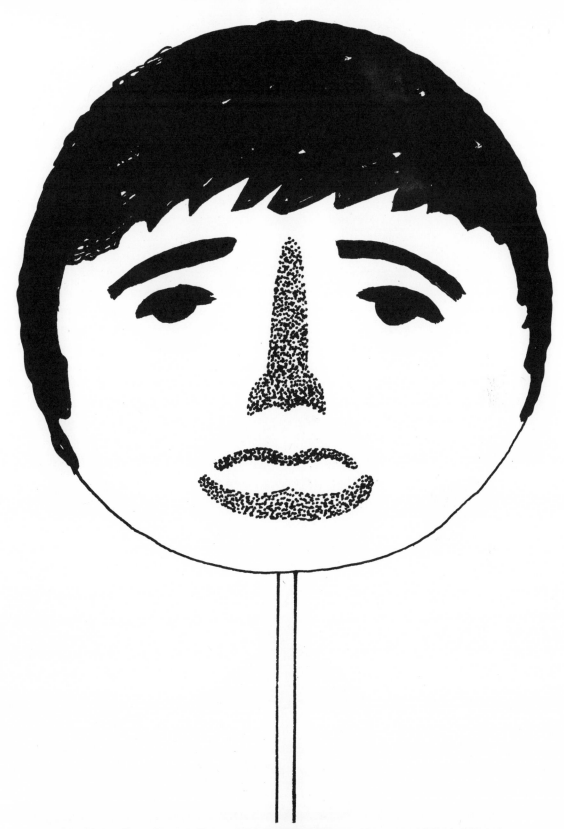

I could eat him all up. Beatle lollipop; white with black hair and eyes, raspberry-pink nose and mouth. Sugar, Corn Syrup, U.S. Certified Colors, Artificial Flavor, Citric Acid. Nt. Wt. 5½ oz. Florence Candy Company, Phila. Pa. Diameter 6 in. United States, 1964

Special pottery is made, censers and candlesticks, and cardboard coffins from which a skeleton jumps when you pull a string. There are candy skulls too with tinsel eyes – death is less alarming when once you have crunched it up between meals. There are whole funeral processions of priests, coffin and mourners going to altars made of paper and chick-peas. Skeletons dance on sticks, there are papier-maché skull masks to wear, clay and wire skeletons with pink paper-fans to pin on, while girls give their lovers skeleton tie-pins with gleaming eyes and dangling legs.

There are also permanent, more ambitious representations of death, less gay, effigies made of wood, or wax or plaster, life-size, glass-eyed, bleeding, bleeding, in countless churches throughout Spain and Portugal and wherever there has been Spanish or Portuguese influence: cruci-fixions, flagellations, crownings with thorns, on altars and walls, in chapels and under little roofs by the roadside. Cupboards are crowded with figures for the holy processions. Open a door, and there they are, blood and tears and pain, real hair, dusty eyelashes, with velvet clothes on bodies made of wood blocks or jointed like dolls. The crosses and instruments of the passion are stored in another cupboard. The wounds may be rubies or paint, or sham blood may flow from a hidden bladder when the nails are struck in. The natives of Latin America took to bloody Christianity like ducks to water: it was just like home. They became expert in making the images, which were so numerous as to warrant production lines, one man sculpting, one gilding, one painting and so on. Assembly was lightning quick, but there might be a dozen priming coats of white paint under the gold leaf or the cheaper yellow ochre. Finally every tear and wound was painted with the utmost realism, and there they still are, in Perpignan or Peru, waiting for the feast days.

NOTES

After the notes to each chapter there is a list of books, some good, all interesting.

INTRODUCTION

1. FRASER, John. *The Aborigines of New South Wales*. Commissioners for the World's Columbian Exposition, 1892.

BENDANN, E. *Death Customs*. Kegan, Paul & Co., London, 1930.
BROWNE, Sir Thomas. *Hydrotaphia or Urne-Buriall*. Many editions, usually with Religio Medici.
CHILDE, Professor Gordon. Directional Changes in Funerary Practices during 50,000 years. *Man*, Sept.–Oct. 1943. Royal Anthropological Institute, London.
CHARON, Jacques. *Death and Western Thought*. Collier Books, New York, 1963.
CRANSTONE, B. A. L. *Melanesia: A Short Ethnography*. The British Museum. London, 1961.
COOPER, G. *I Searched the World for Death*. London, 1940.
The Encyclopaedia of Religion and Ethics (entry on Death and the Disposal of the Dead). Edinburgh, 1910.
GORER, Geoffrey. *Death, Grief, and Mourning in Contemporary Britain*. Cresset Press. London, 1965.
HABENSTEIN, Dr Robert W. and LAMERS, Dr William M.
　　The History of American Funeral Directing. Bulfin Printers Inc. Milwaukee, 1962.
　　Funeral Customs The World Over. Bulfin Printers Inc. Milwaukee, 1962.
HARMER, Ruth. *The High Cost of Dying*. Crowell-Collier Press. New York, 1963.
MITFORD, Jessica. *The American Way of Death*. Hutchinson. London, 1963.
National Association of Funeral Directors. *Manual of Funeral Directing*. London, 1964.
NODES, W. Ltd. *Funeral Guidance*. Printed for private circulation. London, 1931.
PUCKLE, Bertram. *Funeral Customs*. T. Werner Laurie. London, 1926.
PERUCCI, Francesco. *Pompe Funebri Di Tutti Le Nationi*. Verona, 1646.
POLSON, Professor C. J., BRITTAIN, R. B., and MARSHALL, T. K. *The Disposal of the Dead*. English Universities Press. London, 1953. (A very complete run-through of contemporary practice in Great Britain.)
WILLOUGHBY, R. *Funeral Formalities and Obligations*. Universal Publications. London, 1936.
WAUGH, Evelyn. *The Loved One*. Chapman & Hall. London, 1948.

There is an excellent collection of visual material on death under various headings in the Picture Library of New York Public Library.

JOURNALS

The Casket (now incorporated with *The Sunnyside*). Rochester N.Y., 1876.
The Sunnyside (called the *Undertaker* for one year). New York, 1871.
The Undertakers' Journal. Uxbridge, London.
The Western Undertaker (now *The American Funeral Director*), 1879.

THE CORPSE

1. In many early cultures, numerous people and horses were killed at the death of a king, and the Birom and Ibo in Nigeria now import horses specially for this.
2. Natron is native sesquicarbonate of soda. Some authorities say that a saline solution was used; probably practice varied. The Egyptian mummy, when ground into powder, was a favourite and wide-range drug for centuries, probably introduced by the crusaders. Demand outran supply, and new corpses were mummified and sold as Egyptian until the trade was taxed out of existence.

3. From *The Sunnyside,* March 1886.
4. From *The Sunnyside,* April 15th, 1912.
5. From *Archaeologia,* Vol. LX, 1907. On the Funeral Effigies of the Kings and Queens of England. Sir William St John Hope. Vol. LXXXV, 1936. On some later Funeral Effigies in Westminster Abbey. Tanner and Nevinson. Vol. XCVIII, 1961. The Early Royal Funeral Effigies. New Light on Portraiture in Westminster Abbey. Howgrave-Graham.
6. An account of the funeral with photographs was published in *The Illustrated London News* for August 24th, 1957.
7. The Thompson Indians of British Colombia and the Witoto Indians of the N.W. Amazon also have good funeral effigies; the custom is uncommon but widespread. In some Ethiopian graveyards are rows of posts carved with human heads very like the Kafiristan ones, but with all the mouths open.
8. For details of preparation, see the author's *The Unsophisticated Arts,* The Architectural Press. London, 1951.
9. And painted for collections like that at Schloss Ambras, near Innsbruck.

Cairo Museum. *Catalogue Général des Antiquités.* Cairo, 1901.
GEISEY, Ralph E. *The Royal Funeral Ceremony in France.* Geneva, 1960.
HOPE, St John. *Obituary Roll of John Islip, Abbot of Westminster.* Society of Antiquaries. London, 1906.
MAYERS, Eliab. *The Champion Textbook on Embalming.* Champion Chemical Co., Springfield, Ohio, 1908.
RIVET, P. Les Indiens Jibaros. *L'Anthropologie,* XVIII–XIV. XIX 69–87. Paris, 1907.
ROBLEY, Major-General. *Moko, or Maori Tattooing.* London, 1896.
ROBERTSON, Sir George. *The Kafirs of the Hindu-Kush.* Lawrence & Bullen. London, 1896.
STERLING, M. W. Historical and Ethnographical Material on Jivaro Indians. Bureau of American Ethnology, Bulletin 117, Washington, 1938.
UP DE GRAFF, Fritz. *Head Hunters of the Amazon.* Herbert Jenkins. London, 1923.

THE SHROUD

1. *Archaeologia,* Vol. XCVIII.
2. From *Misson on Funerals*; see notes to the Hearse chapter.
3. Walter E. Roth, in the 38th Annual Report of the Bureau of American Ethnology.
4. Larousse, Dictionaire du XIXième siècle, which is very good on funerals generally, giving a useful list of epithets for them; simples, modestes, honorables, illustres, nobles, belles, magnifiques, superbes, pompeuses, solonelles, fastueuses, splendides, guerrières, tristes, lugubres, horribles, sanglantes.
5. From E. Sydney Harland's excellent introduction to the entry on Death in the *Encyclopaedia of Religion,* etc. (see notes to introduction).
6. The Etiquette for Court Mourning. Lady Violet Greville. Supplementary Funeral Number with which is incorporated the ordinary issue, *The Graphic.* Feb. 9th, 1901.
7. From *Etiquette for Ladies,* anonymous, Ward, Lock & Co. London and Melbourne, 1925. Equally rigid rules were laid down for houses; 'Here it may be added that after the funeral the room should be thoroughly aired, and before it is used again, the walls, ceiling and paintwork should be completely redecorated. In the case of the walls, they need to be stripped of all paper and well washed over.' Willoughby (see notes to introduction).
8. From the author's *The Unsophisticated Arts,* see Note 8 above.

BENNET and BIRD. *History of Andean Culture.* American Museum of Natural History.
DAVEY, Richard. *A History of Mourning.* Messrs Jay's, Regent Street, London, undated. This has a charming title-page surrounded by a wreath of the flowers mentioned in Shakespeare's dirges.
d'HARCOURT, Roaul. *Textiles Anciens du Péru.* Paris, 1934.

THE COFFIN

1. Reproduced by kind permission of Messrs B. Weinreb, booksellers, London.

2. A special one was made for the unknown soldier in Westminster Abbey, from one-and-a-half-inch oak, banded in the shape of a cross with forged iron. It has iron rings, and a sword lying on the lid.
3. See the author's *Follies and Grottoes*. Constable. London, 1953.

BRADFORD, C. A. *Heart Burial*. G. Allen & Unwin. London, 1933.

THE HEARSE

1. Cooper-Union Museum, New York, has a good collection of prints and drawings of catafalques.
2. The hearses illustrated on page 103 are, *top left*, a nineteenth century American children's hearse in the Horse n'Buggy Museum, Gettysburg; *top right*, an early twentieth century hearse at Arles, France. *Below*. A mid-nineteenth century English hearse, all wood, the property of W. R. R. Pugh and Sons, Shrewsbury.
3. Reproduced from the author's *The Unsophisticated Arts* by kind permission of the Architectural Press.
4. Very beautiful and elaborate hearses were also used for state funerals in Russia when most other countries had abandoned them. They were (and still are, though no longer baroque) more like gun-carriages than hearses, with the coffin exposed.
5. And also in 1910 a professor of music at Marseilles was buried in her grand piano in a huge grave, and there were current jokes about getting trading stamps with coffins.
6. Sir Richard Steele wrote in 1701 or 2 an amusing play called *The Funeral, or Grief à la Mode*.
7. For collections of trade cards in the British Museum, see notes to chapter on Printing and the Word.

MISSON, Henri. *M. Misson's Memoirs and Observations in his Travels over England*. London, 1719. A charming travel book, with alphabetically arranged comments on English life; beer, buggery, colds, coronations, fish, funerals, scissors, and the table ('blessed be he that invented pudding').

THE FLORAL TRIBUTES

1. The Golden Gates Ajar were made of white helichrysums, and came in three standard sizes: 5 in. by 20 in., $5, 18 in. by 24 in., $7, and 24 in. by 30 in. $10. These are very small compared with the enormous tributes at a rich New York funeral in 1874, where a crowned obelisk was six feet high, and an eagle-capped cross two feet higher.
2. From *The Graphic* Supplementary Funeral Number for February 9th, 1901.

PRINTING AND THE WORD

1. Fuller marketed an earth mined in England near Godstone. It was much used in the late nineteenth and early nineteenth centuries as a skin balm.
2. Two favourite dogs whom he survived a very short time.
3. 'Tract' is reproduced by kind permission of Messrs Macgibbon & Kee Ltd, London, publishers of William Carlos Williams *Collected Earlier Poems*.

BIRRELL, F. F. L. and LUCAS, F. L. *The Art of Dying*. L. & V. Woolf. London, 1930. A good collection of last words.
FENTON, William. *A Portfolio of Railway Notices*. Holland Press, 1964.
LEWIS, John. *Printed Ephemera*. W. S. Cowell. Ipswich, England, 1962.
The Trade Cards of undertakers, coffin-plate-chasers, etc. may be seen in the Heal and Banks collections of trade-cards in the Department of Prints and Drawings in the British Museum, which also has some funeral broadsheets by Catnach and other publishers (good Elegy to Queen Caroline). More funeral ephemera are in Johnson's Sanctuary of Printing, Oxford. Contemporary examples may, of course, be seen by visiting or writing to undertakers, monumental masons, cemeteries, crematoria, specialist printers, etc., and there are sham burial certificates and undertakers' cards in the gift-card shops.

THE PROCESSION

1. PHILLIPPO, James M. *Jamaica: its Past and Present State.* London, 1867. I have been told that at poor funerals in Jamaica today cotton-wool swags may take the place of gold and silver embroidery and carving on the pall and hearse.
2. CASTEAU, F. C. *Guide Des Familles Pour Les Règlements Des Cérémonies Religeuses Et Des Pompes Funèbres.* Paris, 1867.
3. The funeral coach of Sun Yat Sen in 1929 was decorated with stars of pure gold, and for at least the royal funerals wonderful food was made, including elaborately patterned bon-bons.
4. Described in the *Illustrated London News* for January 28th, 1939.
5. See pages 100 and 169. Drawings on pages 100/1 from the sketch books of J. Scharf in the Department of Prints and Drawings, British Museum.
6. Additional MSS 35324, in the Manuscript Room of the British Museum.
7. From Larousse, Dictionaire de XIXième siècle.
8. The wreath is in the Museum of British Transport, Clapham, London, with a fine arrangement of the Royal Train printed in beetroot red, with all the eight coaches carefully drawn.
9. *Illustrated London News.* October 28th, 1939.

COVARRUBIAS, Miguel. *Island of Bali.* Cassel & Co. London, 1937.
The Magnificent and Sumptuous Funeral of Charles V. Antwerp, 1559.

THE CEMETERY

Most cemetery and funeral deities are boringly alike with claws and fangs and rattling skulls. The Voodoo death spirits of Haiti, the large Guédé family, though, have much more style. At the head is a trinity, Baron-Samedi, Baron-la-Croix, and Baron-Cimetière. Baron-Samedi is the particular lord of the many cemeteries, one for each far-reaching family group, and each with the baron's emblem at the gate, a big black cross standing on a false tomb and wearing a top hat and a black frock coat. Another Guédé is Papa-Nebo, a hermaphrodite who may be impersonated by either a male or female hungan in a long white dress and the top hat and black coat, carrying a mattock and a skull, and wearing black spectacles because the dead are blind.

1. *Cambridge Camden Society Tracts.* Cambridge, 1839–1851.
2. Mark Twain, *The Innocents Abroad.* Chatto & Windus. London, many editions.
3. The grotto and the graveyard have been destroyed. A list of the pets' names, with two longer epitaphs, is in the author's *Follies and Grottoes,* Constable. London, 1953.

AUSTIN, E. *Burial Grounds and Cemeteries.* Butterworth & Co. London, 1907.
BERTIN, Georges. *Le Cimetière d'Auteuil.* Tours, 1910.
BLAIR, George. *Biographic and Descriptive Sketches of Glasgow Necropolis.* M. Ogle and Son. Glasgow, 1857.
HOLMES, I. M. *London Burial Grounds.* T. F. Unwin. London, 1896.
HILLAIRET, Jacques. *Les 200 Cimetières du Vieux Paris.* Paris, 1958.
KIRSCH, Johann P. *The Catacombs of Rome.* Rome, 1946.
London Necropolis Company. *Brochure.* London, ?1901.
LOUDON, J. C. On the *Laying-out, Planting, and Managing of Cemeteries,* and on the *Improvement of Churchyards.* London, 1843.
SALA, G. A. *America Revisited,* 1883.
WALKER, George Alfred. *Burial-ground Incendiarism. The Last Fire at the Bone-House in the Spa-Fields Golgotha,* or *The Minute Anatomy of Grave-Digging in London.* London, 1846. *Gatherings from Graveyards,* particularly those of London. London, 1839. *On the past and present state of intramural burying places, with practical suggestions for the establishment of national extramural cemeteries.* London, 1851.

THE TOMB

1. One of the most remarkable tombs in Europe was built for the Emperor Maximilian in the Court Church at Innsbruck; the barest description would take half a chapter – go and see it.

2. Beautiful rubbings of the fierce semi-abstractions of the New England stones have been made by Ann Parker and Avon Neal and published by them from 319 Sixth Avenue, New York.
3. See the author's *Follies and Grottoes*. Constable, London, 1953.
4. The tomb of Sir Richard Burton in the Roman Catholic churchyard at Mortlake, Surrey. The tent is about 14 ft. high, with a star and sun mounted on the roof. Inside it is a painted tent with cherubs on the roof, festoons of camel bells, two tomb-lamps, and two coffins with dusty immortelles.
5. From *Loudon's Cemeteries* (see notes to previous chapter).

EDWARDS, I. E. S. *The Pyramids of Egypt*. Penguin Books. London, 1961.
ESDAILE, Katherine A. *English Church Monuments 1510–1840*. B. T. Batsford. London, 1946.
LINDLEY, Kenneth. *Of Graves and Epitaphs*. Hutchinson. London, 1965. There are a great many more books on tombs than on any other funeral theme – far too many to list.

RELICS AND MEMENTOES

1. I have been told of an embalmed Turk in an English church, and also that there is a mummy called Jimmy Garlick in the church of St James, Garlickhythe, London, but I have not been able to verify these in time for press.
2. There is a persistent story that Queen Victoria had a dummy of Prince Albert to dine with and talk to.
3. See pages 167 and 172.
4. Notably Louis XIV and Marie Antoinette. There is a good one of Robespierre in the Carnavalet Museum, Paris. Probably the best-known death mask is L'Inconnue de la Seine, the girl found in the Paris morgue who smiled blindly in so many studios and drawing-rooms at the turn of the century. For details of the manufacture of masks and wax-works, see the author's *Unsophisticated Arts*.
5. And a marvellous tableau of the inhabitants of Messina dying of the plague, by Gaetano Zumbo, is in the Bargello in Florence.

BENTHAM, Jeremy. *Auto-Icon*. London, 1832.
LAWTON, Harry. *Willie-Boy*. Paisano Press. U.S.A. 1960.
MARMOY, C. F. A. The Auto-Icon of Jeremy Bentham at University College, London. Reprint from *Medical History* Vol. 2, No. 2, April, 1958. University College, London, undated.

WHERE DEATH GETS YOU

1. See Tebb, below.
2. From the *London Morning Leader,* probably 1909.
3. See Tebb, below.
4. From *The Sunnyside*, August 14th, 1875.
5. See RATTRAY, *Religion and Art in Ashanti*. Oxford, 1927.
6. See notes to chapter on The Cemetery.
7. JARVIS, W. John. *The Glyptic*. J. R. Smith. London, 1875.
8. From *Science Siftings* (U.S.A.). March 16th, 1901.

TEBB, William, F.R.G.S. and VOLLUM, Col. E. P., M.D. *Premature Burial*. Swan Sonnenschein & Co. Ltd. London, 1905. Second edition.
SNART, John. *Thesaurus of Horror*. London, 1817.

LOVING DEATH

1. From the *Hampstead and Highgate Gazette*, London.
2. From a contemporary newspaper, no heading, no date.
3. Bad artists like grue too; see for instance the Musée Wiertz in Brussels, where all Antoine Wiertz's huge horror canvases are kept.

4. A very full list is in the illustrated catalogue of the sale of Susan Minns' collection on the Dance of Death, 1922.
5. See p. 248. Teeth used to be kept to bury with the corpse; these were probably the result of several such collections, forgotten and later put to good use.
6. Copies of some of the engravings are in the British Museum and the Wellcome Institute, London.

CALI, François. *The Art of the Conquistadores.* Thames & Hudson. London, 1961.
COLE, F. J. *A History of Comparative Anatomy.* Macmillan & Co. London, 1944. A good account of the loving anatomical engravings of the 16th and 17th centuries – Ruysch, Coiter, Casserius, Swammerdam, etc.
DAVENPORT, Marcia. A fiction-non-fiction account of the Collyer brothers.
DIAZ, Bernal. *The Conquest of Mexico.* Penguin Books. London.
MEXICAN FOLKWAYS. October–November, 1927.
TOOR, Frances. *A Treasury of Mexican Folkways.* Crown, New York, 1947.
VAILLANT, G. C. *The Aztecs.* Penguin Books. London, 1950. The Aztecs and the people of Benin probably carried the cult of bloody death further than anyone else. For Dahomey, see J. A. Skertchley's *Dahomey As It Is.* Chapman & Hall. London, 1874.

ANGLO-AMERICAN QUIZ-GAME

The five long epitaphs, and the short ones through *Alas Poor Fanny* to the end, are all English.

INDEX

Abney Park Cemetery, 179
Afghanistan. *See* Kafiristan
Alaskan tombs, 227
All Saints Day, 291
American Civil War: establishes embalmer's art, 23; rubber interment sacks used in, 73
Ananda, King of Thailand, 174–5
Animals: mummified, in Ancient Egypt, 48, 54; shrouds for, 62; cemeteries for, 193–7; epitaphs to, 151
Animal-shaped coffins, 70, 92
Anne of Bohemia, 40
Anne of Denmark, 40
Anthropoid coffins, 74, 93
Arlington Military Cemetery, 191, 192
Art-work, on corpses, 22
Arterial embalming, 22
Ashanti funerary customs, 125, 265
Australian Bushman's funeral procession, 158
Austria: mourning in, 63; snake symbol from, 215
Aviero Cemetery, Portugal, 186, 187, 189, 219

Baden-Powell, Lord, 265
Bakuba tribal relic, 255
Bali: death-size dolls, 47, 48; coffins, 90–2; funeral processions, 163
Baluchistan, stone tomb in, 202
Banz, reliquaries at, 240
Baralino, Carlo, 182
Baroque hearses, 99–100
Batalha, Portugal, shrine in monastery at, 253
Bead-work immortelles, 132
Beatle, lollipops, 292–3
Becket, Thomas à, 244
Benin, ancestor-figure from, 254
Bentham, Jeremy, 244–5
Black horses, bred for funeral trade, 100
Blakeston, Oswell, quoted, 261
Blot, Henri, 278
Bones. *See* Skeletons
Bramber, Sussex, Potter's Museum at, 270
Bridgnorth, Shropshire, tomb at, 215
Brightling, Sussex, tomb at, 208
Brompton Cemetery, 179
Brookwood Cemetery, 181–2
Browne, Sir Thomas, 155; *Urne Buriall*, 57
Buckingham, Duchess of, 45
Buenos Aires, carved hearse, 96
Buffalo, N.Y., mausoleum, 222–4
Burgos, Spain, reliquary at, 243
Burial methods, 9–10
Burma: coffins, 70, 91; hearses, 106
Burton, Sir Richard, tomb of, 225

Cabaret du Néant, 261–3
Calaveras, 286–91
Cambridge Camden Society, 179
Cameroons, calabash from, 94
Camillo de Lellis, San, 235
Carisbrooke Castle, I.o.W., 246
Carved animals, corpses burned in, 91–2
Casket, The, 142, 146
Caskets, 74, 79–81; furniture for, 82–3; cremation caskets, 84; for mausoleum burial, 84
Castle Howard, Yorks., tombs at, 214
Castro, Inez de, 261
Catacombs, 178–9, 280, 282–4
Catafalque, 98
Cemeteries, 177–201; English, 178–82; Père-Lachaise, 182, 183, 199; Staglieno, Italy, 182, 184–6; Aviero, Portugal, 186–7, 189; American, 189–93; for animals, 193–7; lawn cemeteries, 198–9
Cerberus, 21
Charles I, 45, 246
Charles II, 45
Charles VI (of France), 45
Charles VII (of France), 45
Charles VIII (of France), 45
Charon, 21
Cheops, Great Pyramid of, 203
Chesterfield, Foljambe tomb at, 205
Children: child's coffin, 89; white hearses for their funerals, 101
China: colours for death, 53; social status and the coffin, 73; funeral processions, 163
Chionski, Anthony de, 258
Christians, early, funeral customs of, 111
Churchill, Sir Winston, 250
Churchyards, 177–8
City of London Cemetery and Crematorium, Manor Park, 128, 181, 199
Clay pipe, in shape of skull, 266
Clouet, François, 46
Coachman's mourning cockade, 65
Coffin, Hayden, his tooth-powder, 273–4
Coffins, 71, 73; oriental, 70, 90–2; American, 73–84; African, 93–4; European, 72, 75, 78–9, 85; handles and nailheads for, 86–7; linings for, 88; child's coffin, 89; Haden's speedier decay coffins, 263; O'Kelley's air coffin, 275
Collyer, Langley and Homer, 277–8
Colours for death, 53
Colt, Maximilian, 44, 207
Columbarium, 199, 205
Columbian mummy, 14
Compton, Surrey, mausoleum at, 214

Corpses, keeping of, 14, 21, 244–5
Corpus Christi funeral, 159
Costers' funeral procession, 166–7
Crandall, Joel E., 23, 25
Crape, 64, 66
Cremation: in ancient Greece, 22; urns for, 176, 200
Crematoria, 181–2, 199, 201
Criminals' relics, 253
Cromwell, Oliver, 45
Croydon, horse-drawn hearse in, 107
Crucifixion, 278

Dance of Death, 279–80
Day of the Dead, in Mexico, 286–91
Death masks, 250, 253
Derby, Alice Countess of, crest on tomb of, 207
Dia de los Muertos. *See* Day of the Dead
Dogon tribe (Sudan), effigies preside at funerals of, 46
Donne, John, tomb of, 57, 59
Dunbar, *Lament for the Makers,* 279
Durham Cathedral, 186
Dying, 16–20

Ear-rosette, funeral horse's, 102
Ear-trumpet, for full mourning, 68
Easter Island, 122
Edward I, 57
Edward III, 40
Edward IV, 40
Effigies of the dead: ancient Rome, 22; English, 39, 40, 44–58; Bentham, 245; French and Italian, 45–6; in Bali and Kafiristan, 47–9; modern, 250, 253
Egypt, Ancient, 122; burial customs, 20–1, 22, 73; mummified animals, 48, 54; funeral trades, 111; the pyramids, 203–5
Elizabeth I, Queen, 45; funeral procession of, 167, 170–1
Elizabeth of York (queen of Henry VII), effigy of, 40, 42, 44
Embalming: Ancient Egypt, 20, 21, 48, 53, 73; ancient Roman, 22; arterial, 22; modern American, 22–3, 25–7; mediaeval English, 40; of animals, 48, 54; Colleges of, 145–6
Empty Chairs, 124, 125
Entrails, 21, 284–6
Epitaphs. *See* Tomb inscriptions
Escorial, mausoleum at the, 206, 214
Euphemisms for death, 152, 155
Evisceration, 21–2
Evora, Portugal, bone chapel at, 279–81

Face-former, 24

Fali tribe (Nigeria), burial wrapping of, 55
False tail, of funeral horse, 102
Feather bird tribute, 128
Feather tray and feather-pages, 100, 167, 168
Fisk, Almond, his metallic coffin, 74, 75
Floral tributes, 119–32
Flower-cards, 136
Forest Lawn Memorial Park, California, 191
France: royal effigies, 45–6; undertakers, 113, 114; immortelles, 132; funeral processions, 160, 161; cemeteries, 182, 183, 188
François I, 46
French Congo, anthropoid coffin from, 93
Frères de la Charité, Les, 114
Freshl, A., his patent drapes, 71, 74
Frogmore, Windsor, 214
Fuller, Mad Jack, tomb of, 208
Funeral cards. See Memorial cards
Funeral cars, 99
Funeral literature, 146–7. See also Trade papers; Memorial cards
Funeral procession, 159–75

Gaillard, Claude, 199
Genoa, Staglieno Cemetery at, 182, 184–6
Gettysburg Cemetery, 191
Gipsies, burial customs of, 99
Golden Gates, 121
Golders Green Crematorium, 199
Gondola funeral. See Water funeral
Gothic Revival, 99
Graphic, 147
Grasso, G. V., 185
Great Barrington, Mass., tomb at, 221
Greece, ancient: burial customs, 21–2; tombs, 205
Griaule, Professor, 46
Grosjean's Funeral Annunciator, 64, 66
Guillamot (architect), 178

Haden, Seymour, his speedier decay coffins, 263
Hair, kept as memento of the dead, 246–7
Halicarnassus, tomb of Mausolus at, 206
Harefield, Middx, tombs at, 207
Hartsdale Canine Cemetery, N.Y., 194, 196–7, 201
Harvey, William, 22
Hauterives, France, tomb at, 218
Hawksmoor, Nicholas, 214
Hearse: old styles, 97–104; motor hearse, 96, 105–10
Heart burial or preservation, 92, 95
Henri IV, 45
Henrietta Maria, 44
Henry I, 40
Henry II, 40
Henry III, 40

Henry V, 40, 45
Henry VII, 40, 44
Henry Prince of Wales, effigy of, 43, 44
Herodotus, 21, 203
Highgate Cemetery, 179–81
Hoby, Lady, effigy of, 58
Holbein, Hans, 279
Holmes, Mrs Basil, 265–6
Horses, bred for funeral trade, 100, 101
Hugo, Victor, 172
Hunter, Dr William, 22

Ilford, Essex, Pets' Cemetery at, 193, 195
Immortelles, 129–30, 132
Inscriptions. See Tomb inscriptions
Invitations to funerals, 135
Isfahan, 186
Italy: coffins, 85; funeral processions, 160, 161; cemeteries, 182, 184–6; catacombs, 280–4

James I, 44
Japan: colours for death, 53; Shinto funerals, 163
Jaw of deceased, as memento, 249
Jericho, skulls from, 37
Jewellery: kept as a memento, 246; mourning jewellery, 246–8
Jivaro Indians, death's heads of, 37–9
Jones, Henry, his Musée Phusée Glyptic, 270
Josat, M., 272

Kafiristan, Afghanistan, wooden effigies of, 48, 49
Karnicé-Karnicki, Count, 258–60
Katherine de Valois, 40–1
Kensal Green Cemetery, 179, 181
Kissing the dead hand, 261
Kittens, in tableaux-morts, 268, 270

Landseer, Sir Edwin, 270
Larousse, quoted, 64
Lawn cemeteries, 198–9
Lenin, 235
Leningrad, wax effigy of Peter the Great in the Hermitage, 46
Lermoos, Austria, tomb at, 206
Lettering, 83, 97, 112, 126–7, 135, 148
Letters of condolence, 141
Lexington, Mass., tomb at, 209
Life-casts, 250
Lincoln, Abraham, 172
Lisbon: Jewish Cemetery, 191; relics in church of Madre de Deus, 240–2
Livingstone, David, 95
London, 166, 178, 179
London Necropolis Co., 181–2
Louisiana Rural Cemetery, 228
Lowenburg, Silesia, tomb at, 221
Lyre with broken strings, 118

Mahon, Patrick, 253

Manor Park. See City of London Cemetery and Crematorium
Marx, Karl, 181
Mary Tudor, 40
Mary II, 45, 98
Masks. See Death masks
Massachusetts College of Embalming, 23
Mausoleum burial, 206, 214, 222–3; caskets for, 84
Mausolus, tomb of, 206
Mazzini, Giuseppe, 185
Mementos of the dead, 246–55
Memorial cards, 135–41
Mexico: Day of the Dead in, 27, 286–91; symbols on graves, 119, 133; church image-makers of, 244; sugar skull, 277
Mimes, 261
Monumental mason, 113, 117
Mortuaries, 257–8
Motor hearse, 105–8
Mourning, 62–9
Mourning jewellery, 247–8
Mummies. See Embalming
Munich, Waiting Mortuaries in, 257
Murcia Cathedral, parchment skeleton in, 286
Museums, 50–1, 270
Mutes, 100, 167, 261

Naples, funeral processions in, 159, 161
Napoleon I, 171–2
Necrophilia, 278
Nelson, Lord, 45, 171
'Never laugh when a ghost goes by' (poem), 266
New Guinea, skull from, 30
New Hebrides, skull from, 28
New Ireland, skull from, 33
New York, cemeteries in, 189, 190
New Zealand, preserved head from, 35
Nigeria. See Fali tribe
Nipple-pincers, 272
Norfolk, 178
Northampton, Lady, 171
Norwood Cemetery. See West Norwood

Oak coffins, 85
Oatlands Park, Surrey, 193
Oberammergau, reliquary at, 236–7
O'Kelley, James M., his Navohi invention, 275
Order of Service, 136, 141
Ossuaries, 278–84
Outina tribe, corpse mutilation, 20

Paid mourners, 261
Palermo, catacombs in, 284
Paper figures, in funeral processions, 162, 163
Pappalardo, Aurelio, quoted, 284
Papua, skull from, 32. See also Western Papua
Paré, Ambrose, 92

Pargetter's hearse, 106
Paris: its catacombs, 178–9; Père-Lachaise Cemetery, 182, 183, 199, 227; Montparnasse Cemetery, 215; *Salles des Martyres* at 1935 Exhibition, 235
Pearly King or Queen, funeral procession of, 166–7
Pearly Gates, 125, 134
Pedro, King of Portugal, 261
Peoria, Illinois, 23
Père-Lachaise Cemetery. *See* Paris
Peruvian mummy-bundle, 53, 56
Peter the Great, 284
Pets, epitaphs to, 151. *See also* Animals
Phusiglyptic sculpture, 270
Pisa, Campo Santo at, 186
Pitt, William, 45
Plastic flowers and wreaths, 132
Pop art, 286
Portraits of the dead, 22
Portugal: coffins, 89–90; hearses, 104–5, 109–10; tombs, 148, 219, 232; announcements, 153–4; cemeteries, 186–7, 189, 191, 219
Potter, Walter. *See* Bramber
Premature Burial, 257–60, 212–13
Pyramids, 203–5

Raccolta Miani, 51
Raleigh, Sir Walter, 171
Rastrelli, 46
Registers, of those who sent flowers, 141
Relics and reliquaries, 235–44
Renard, tomb of Chevalier and Mme, 227
Richmond, Duchess of (La Belle Stuart), 45
Romans, ancient: burial customs, 22; heart burial or preservation, 92; funeral trades, 111; tombs, 205; death masks, 250
Rome, City of: wax effigy in S. Maria della Vittoria, 46; relics in Santa Maria Maddelena, 235; catacombs of the Capuchin Fathers, 280, 282–4
Rubber interment sacks, 73–4
Ruysch, Fredrik, his museum of corpses, 284–6

St Etienne, overstuffed hedgehog in Industrial Museum at, 51
St Roque, Portugal, relics in church of, 244
Salt, Sir Titus and Lady, 214
Saltaire, Yorks., mausoleum at, 214
Schloss Ambras, Austria, skeleton at, 278–9

Schnitger, Dr F. M., 166
Scotland: coffins, 85; tombs, 178
Sea, burial at, 85
Sebastian, St, 278
Seine, animal cemetery on island in the, 193
Shinto funerals, 163
Shorwell, I.o.W., tombs at, 213
Shrewsbury, Gothic hearse at, 99
Shrouds, 53–62
Shrunken heads. *See* Tsantsas
Sin-eating, 261
Skeletons, 235–45, 264, 271, 275–91
Skulls, 12–13, 25, 27–37, 56, 238–9, 245, 249, 266–7
Smith, Southwood, 244–5
Smuts, General, 174
Snart, John, *Thesaurus of Horror*, 272–3
Solomon Islands: skull from 34; reliquary from, 238–9
Souvenirs. *See* Mementos
Soyer, Alexis, 147
Spain: coffins, 85; funeral processions, 160; tombs, 206, 214; reliquaries, 240, 243
Staglieno. *See* Genoa
Stalin, J., 174
State funerals, 167, 170–5
Stevens and Bean's Automorgue-mobile, 106
Stockholm, Biological Museum, 50
Stratford-on-Avon, Musée Phusée Glyptic at, 270
Styka, Jan, 191
Sugar skull, 276
Sumatra, processions, 163–6
Sunnyside, The, 135, 141–6
Sutherland, Duke of, 263
Symbols of death, 11

Tableaux-morts, 268, 270
Tahiti, mourning costume from, 67
Taxidermy, 48–51. *See also* Tableaux-morts
Thompson's hearse, 106
Tobacco-jar, in shape of skull, 267
Tomb inscriptions, 147–51, 229
Tombs: stone tomb in Baluchistan, 202; Egyptian pyramids, 203–5; Greek and Roman, 205; early Christian and mediaeval, 205; English, 206–8, 210–13; mausoleums, 206, 214; 19th and 20th centuries, 214–18; modern symbolism, 229; headstones, mousetraps and curbs, 229–32; planting on graves, 233
Torres Straits, skull from, 29
'Tract' (poem), 155–7
Trade papers, undertakers', 141–6
Trefriw, N. Wales, tombs at, 226

Trompe l'oeil postcard, 12
Tsantsas (Jivaro heads), 37, 39
Turkey, colours for death in, 53; flowers on graves, 233
Tussaud's, Madame, 250, 253
Twain, Mark, on Staglieno Cemetery, 182, 184, 186
Tytler, Mary Fraser, 214

Undertakers, 110–17; benevolent society, 114; visiting cards, 141; trade papers, 141–6
Urns, for heart burial, 92. *See also* Cremation urns
Ursula, St, 278

Vancouver, tombstone at, 233
Venice: Museo da Storia Naturale, 50–1; water funerals in, 99, 161
Vesalius, 278
Victoria, Queen, 122, 147, 172–3
Visiting cards, undertakers', 141

Wailers, 261
Waiting Mortuaries, 257–8
Wales: coffins, 85; churchyards, 178; tombs, 214, 226; sin-eating in, 261
Walker, G. A., *Gatherings from Graveyards*, 178
War relics, 253
Watchers, 261
Warter, Yorks., mausoleum at, 214
Washington, D.C., military cemetery at. *See* Arlington
Water funerals, 99, 161
Watts, G. F., 214
Wax effigies. *See* Effigies
Wellington, Duke of, funeral of, 172; lying-in-state of, 246
West Indies, funeral processions in, 160–1
West Norwood Cemetery, 179
West Wycombe, Bucks, Dashwood mausoleum at, 95, 214
Western America, 151
Western Papua: decorated head from, 31; stuffed head from, 36
Westminster Abbey, 41, 44–5
White, John, 105
Whitehead, Paul, 95
Widows, mourning period for, 64, 69
William II (Rufus), 40
William III, 45
Willie Boy, 235, 253
Wire frames: for crosses, 123; for the Empty Chair, 124
Woking Crematorium, 181, 199
Wreaths. *See* Floral tributes

Zoser, step pyramid of, 204